How to Draw
NeoPopRealism
color abstract IMAGES

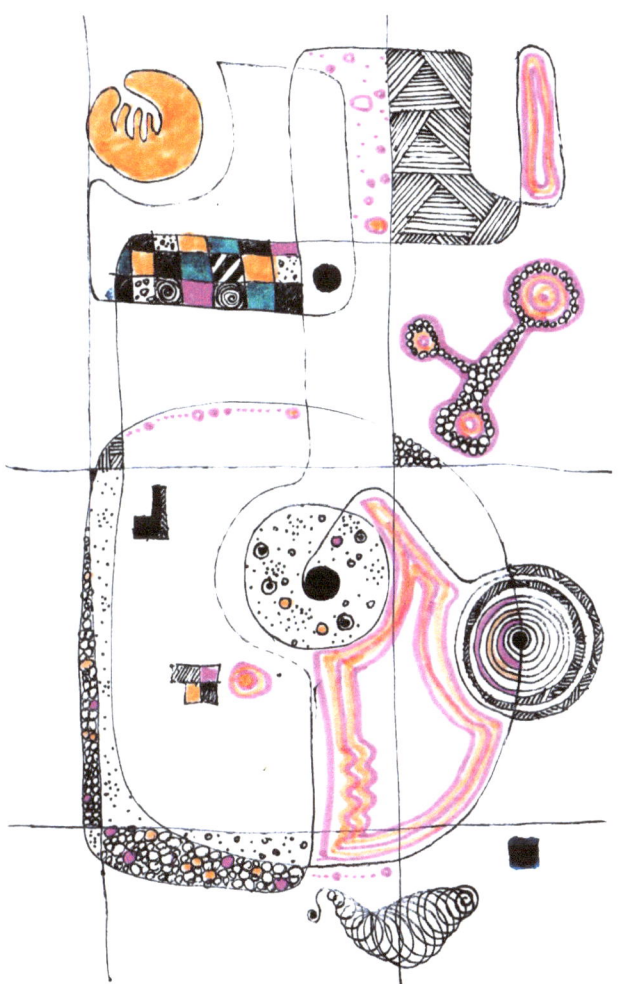

Ink Backgrounds

NADIA RUSS
NeoPopRealism PRESS

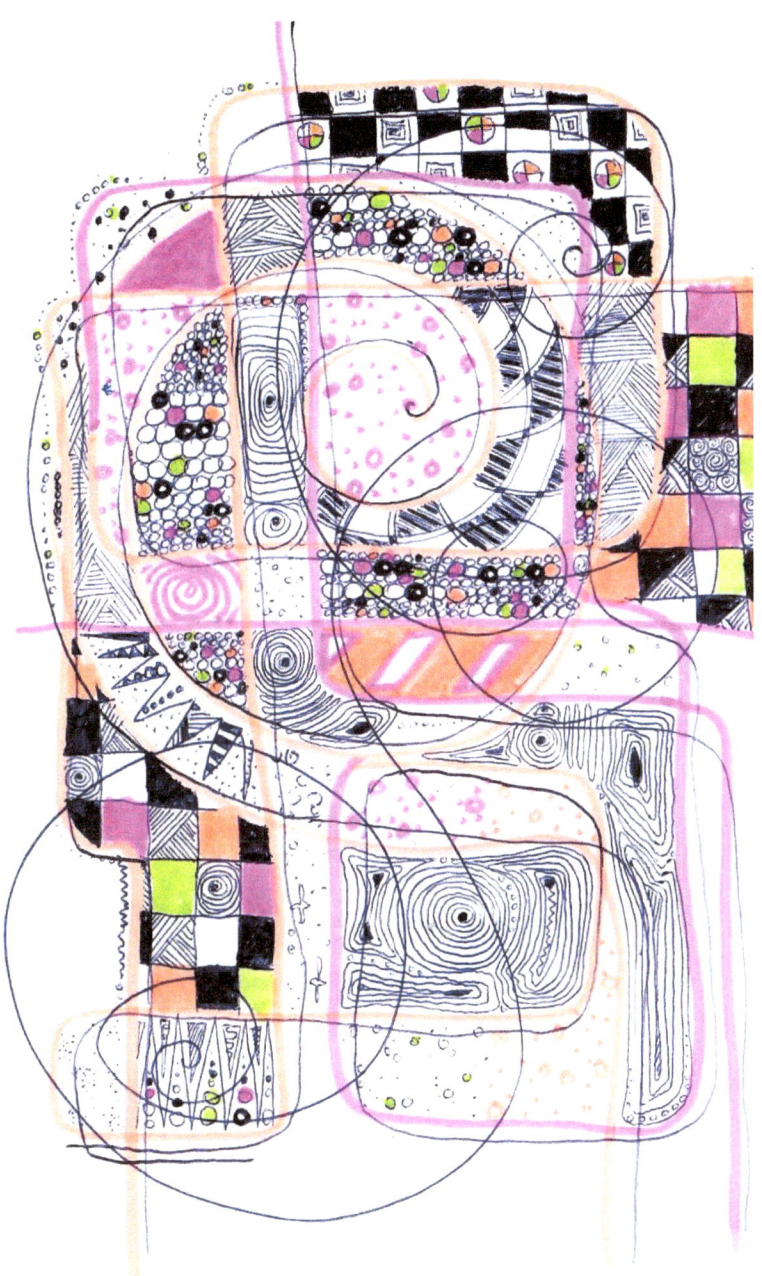

Abstract 7, *Meditation*, black Ink & color marker on paper

NeoPopRealism ink backgrounds are whimsical, they are simple and complicated at the same time.

How to Draw

NeoPopRealism

color abstract IMAGES

Ink Backgrounds

NADIA RUSS

NeoPopRealismPRESS

First time published in 2011 by NeoPopRealism PRESS
PO BOX 366
New York, NY 10013

NeoPopRealismPRESS@mail.com

"How to Draw NeoPopRealism Color Abstract Images: Ink Backgrounds" by Nadia RUSS.
Illustrated by Nadia RUSS.

ISBN-13: 9780615581804
ISBN-10: 0615581803

11 12 13 14 15   10 9 8 7 6 5 4 3 2 1

Published in the United States of America
Language: English

This book teaches how to draw NeoPopRealism color abstracts / ink backgrounds.

For teenagers and adults

www.neopoprealism.org

CONTENT

INTRODUCTION

NeoPopRealism ink drawing concept was created by Nadia Russ in 1989. It was an experiment. She was trying to connect to the Universe and let the Universe use her as a Conductor when she created her drawings. She didn't want to follow any other artists' achievements, she decided to create absolutely new art form, like Picasso (Cubism), Dali (Surrealism), Andy Warhol (Pop Art) and a few other worldwide known artists had done.

Nadia Russ took her ink pen and began to draw a flowing line that turned into shapes, figures, often faces. Then, some sections (or all), that appeared, she filled with the repetitive patterns. She never uses eraser because if a mistake made, it disappears with the following repetitive patterns that balance the whole composition. Her work was unique; no one did anything like this before.

Later, January 4, 2003, Nadia Russ created a word NeoPopRealism and internationally announced new style of visual arts.

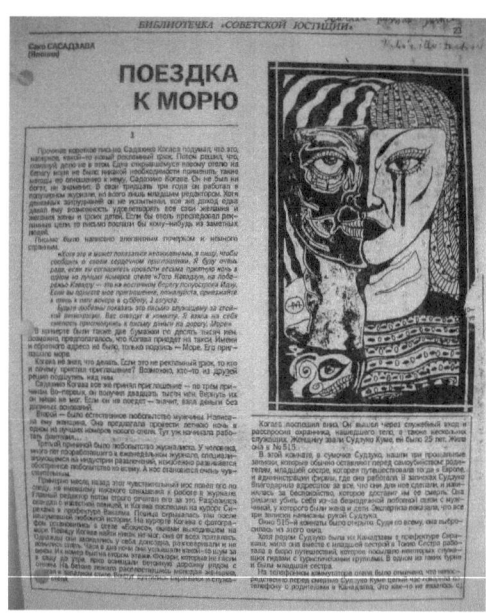

Nadia Russ illustrated a story by Saho Sasadzava for the *Russian Justice* Journal, 1992, Moscow, Russia

Get inspired

Your initial view is probably too conventional and full of prejudice and assumption.

When you focus on success, you fall into the trap of comparing yourself to others, feeling envious. Instead, focus on getting better every day, focus on excellence. Gratitude floods your body and brain with emotions that uplift and energize you. Use your strengths for a bigger purpose beyond yourself. Focus on what you are giving instead of what you are getting, it makes every your step more rewarding and meaningful.

Your artwork is reflection of you, your moods; also it depends on what your artistic task is. Albert Einstein said that "imagination is more important than knowledge. Knowledge is limited. Imagination encircles the world." Your Imagination forms new images that have not been previously experienced; it is free from objective restraints. The world as you experience it is an interpretation of your senses. Some cultures and traditions view the dreams as reality, as Australian Aborigines… When you draw your NeoPopRealism backgrounds, you use your imagination. This drawing can be light or very busy, with the complicated-looking, whimsical ornaments, where line twists and turns seemed unpredictably. The drawing of the busy abstracts/backgrounds is meditative process. The meditative state of mind is the highest state in which our mind can exists. When you draw your whimsical images, your mind is open for the renewal. And more you draw, more relaxed you are. The repetitive patterns' drawing process invites you to the world where everything is simple as the sun and sky, and you are mesmerized by this simplicity and by the drawing process itself.

After you finish one pattern, you begin draw anther, and so on. The images look complicated, but not all are that complicated when you start execute them. Concept is: *Line creates sections; sections fill with the repetitive patterns, using ink pen. You never use eraser.* With this drawing method you can achieve not only interesting artistic results, but also the purity of your mind. It is like a journey to the world of unknown with good feeling, knowing that you can turn the complexity into simplicity. This drawing is intuitive. Believe in yourself: you are a magician who can execute magic with the ink pen. You need no eraser because if a 'mistake' made, it disappears with the following repetitive patterns that balance the whole composition. Isn't that magic?

Use ink pens *Foray Rolle Rollerball Medium 0.7 mm, Sharpie* or any similar and the color markers. You can draw on cardstock paper 8.5"x11" or any other type or size of paper, depending on your artistic tasks and projects. The following abstracts made on pieces of paper 5.5"x8.5". To get this size of paper simply cut cardstock 8.5"x11" into two same size pieces.

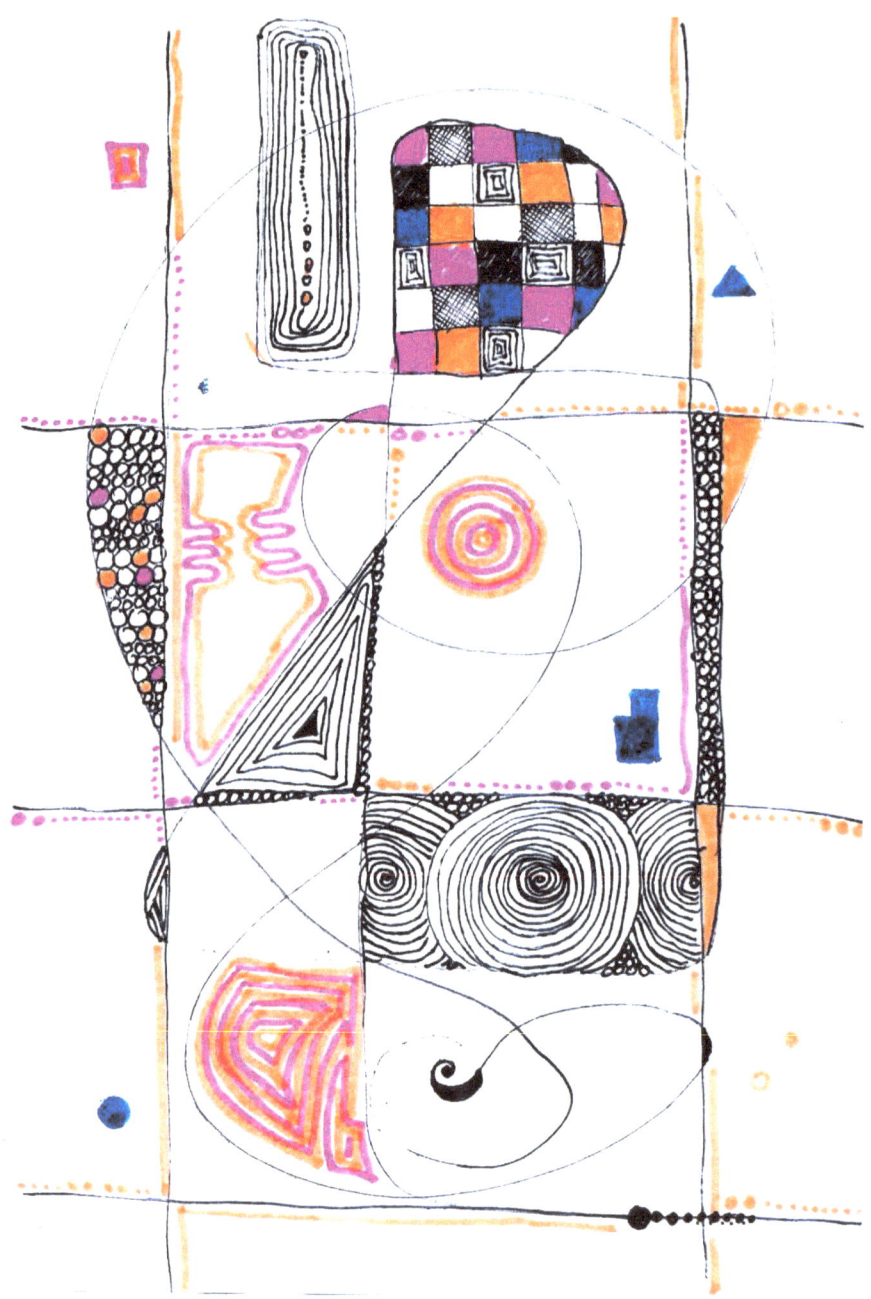

Abstract 6, Meditation, black ink pen & color marker on paper

How to create NeoPopRealist color Abstract 1

The following pages will show you step-by-step how to create the color abstract, which can be used as the background for NeoPopRealism ink artwork that contains faces, figures or other objects. Also you can use such abstracts as independent graphic designs. Learn to improvise. Improvisation is a creative process without the prior preparation, like the Jazz in music. It will lead you to the discovery and will help your creative flow.

Each following image includes new detail(s). The complete image looks like this:

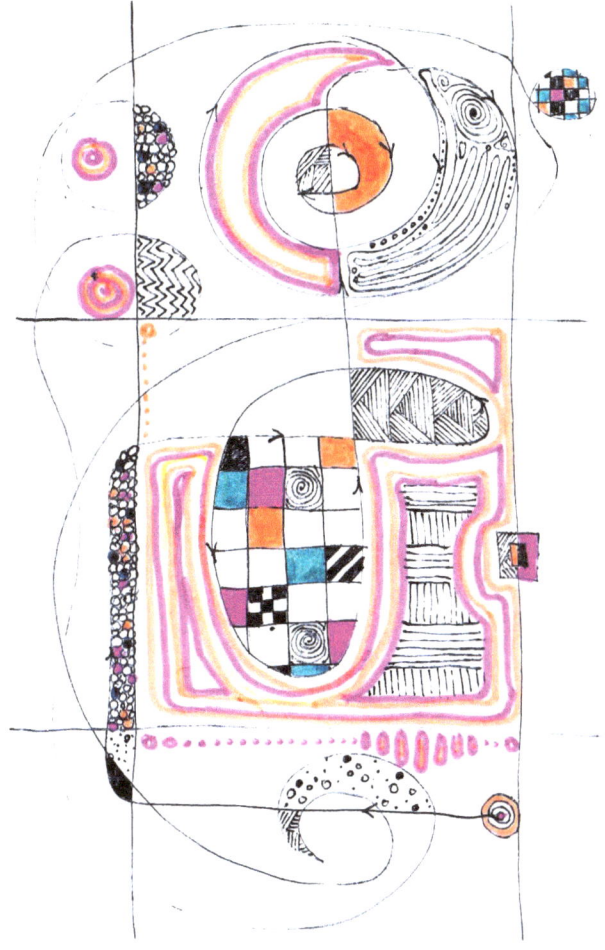

Abstract 1, Meditation, black ink pen & color markers on paper

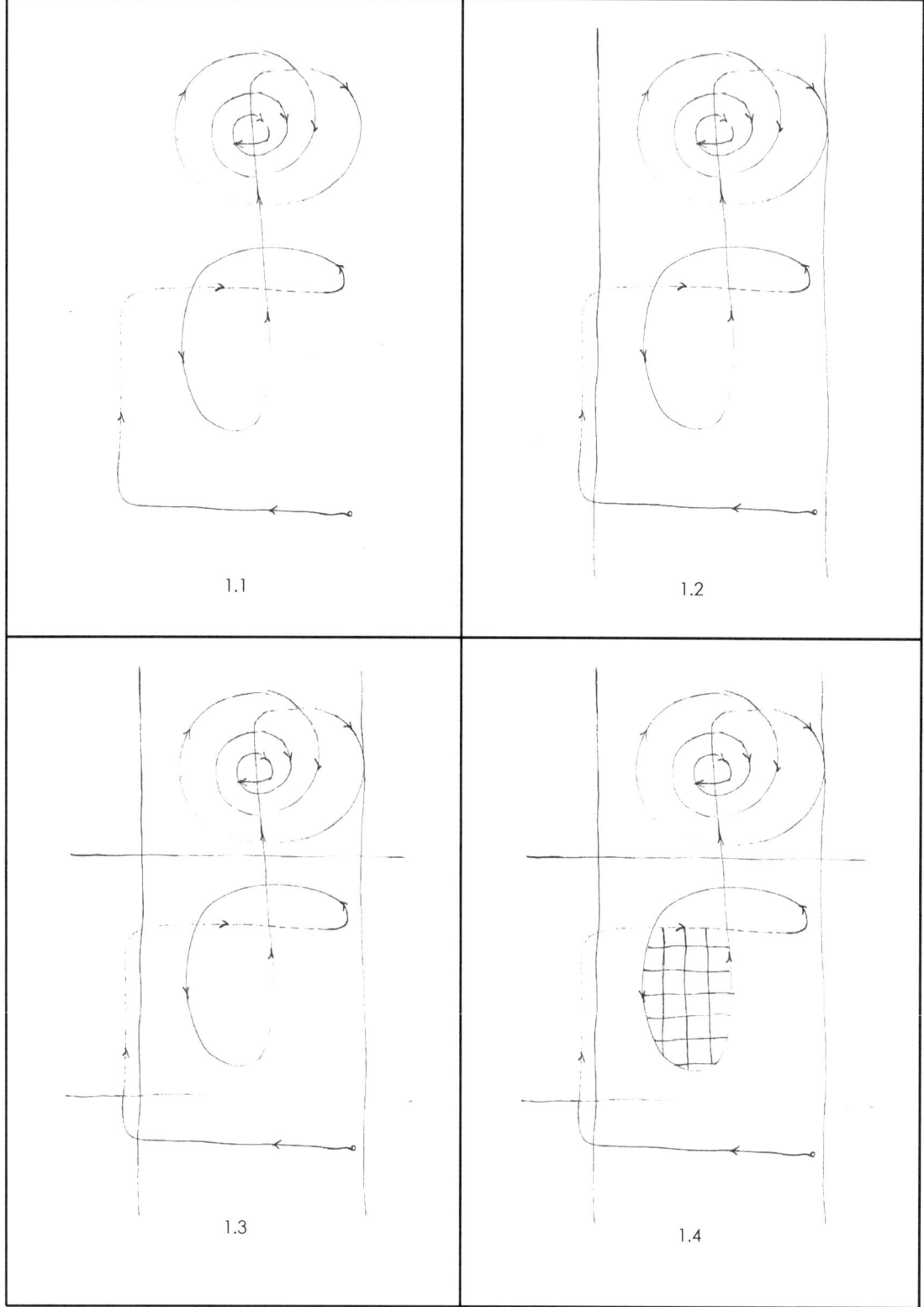

1.1

1.2

1.3

1.4

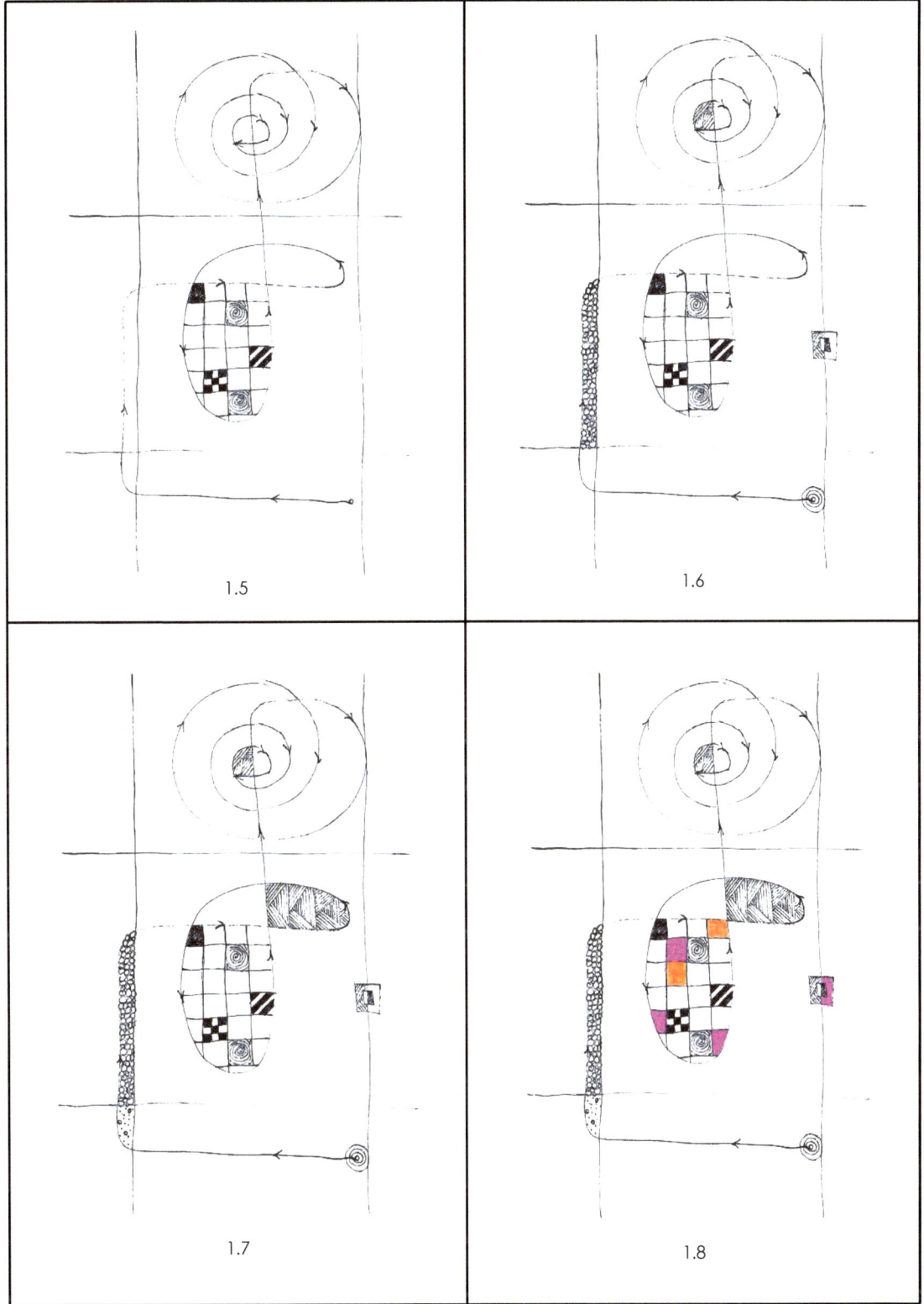

1.5

1.6

1.7

1.8

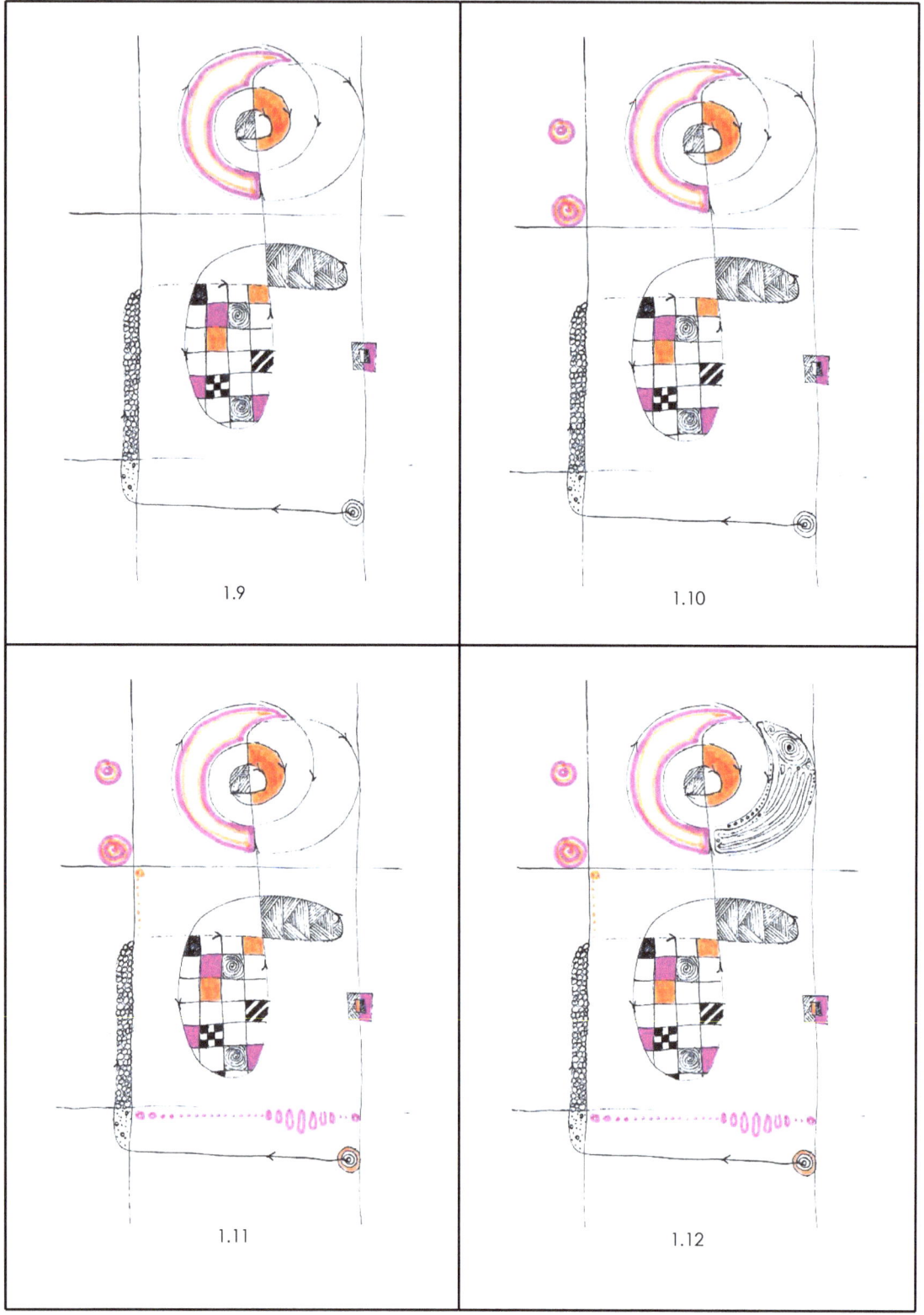

1.9

1.10

1.11

1.12

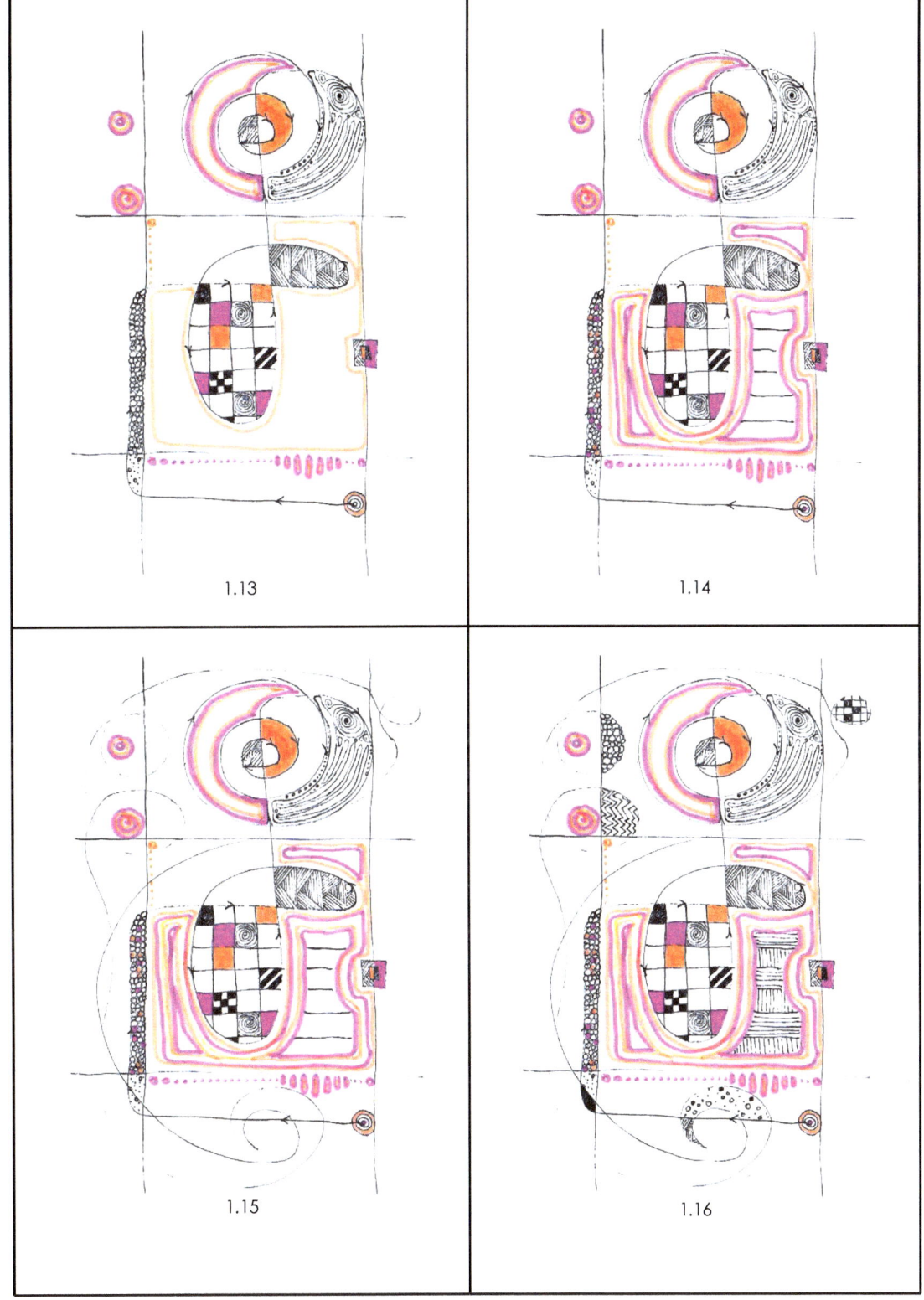

1.13

1.14

1.15

1.16

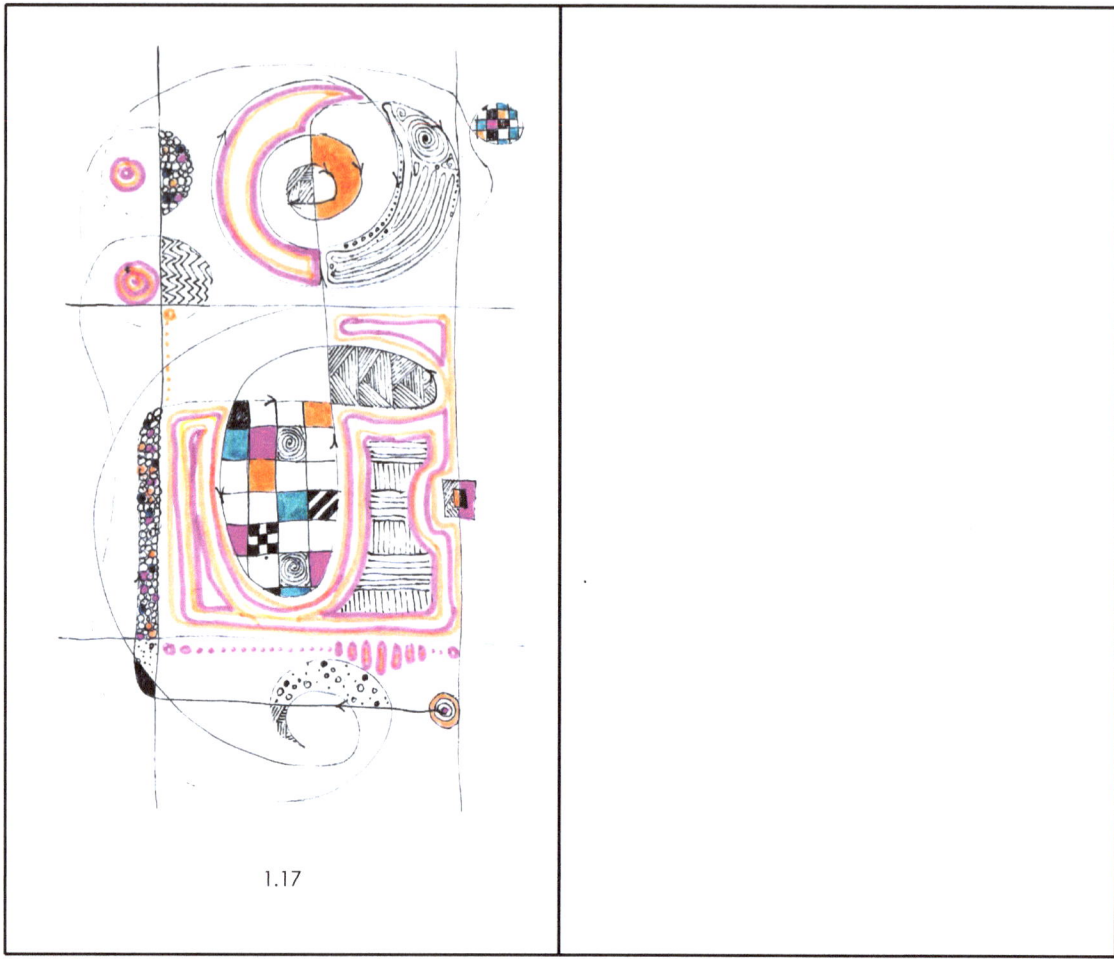

1.17

The complicated looking drawings are made out of simple patterns. The following pages (17-19) will show you how to draw repetitive patterns, used in NeoPopRealism *Abstract 1*. Each following image of the particular pattern includes new detail(s).

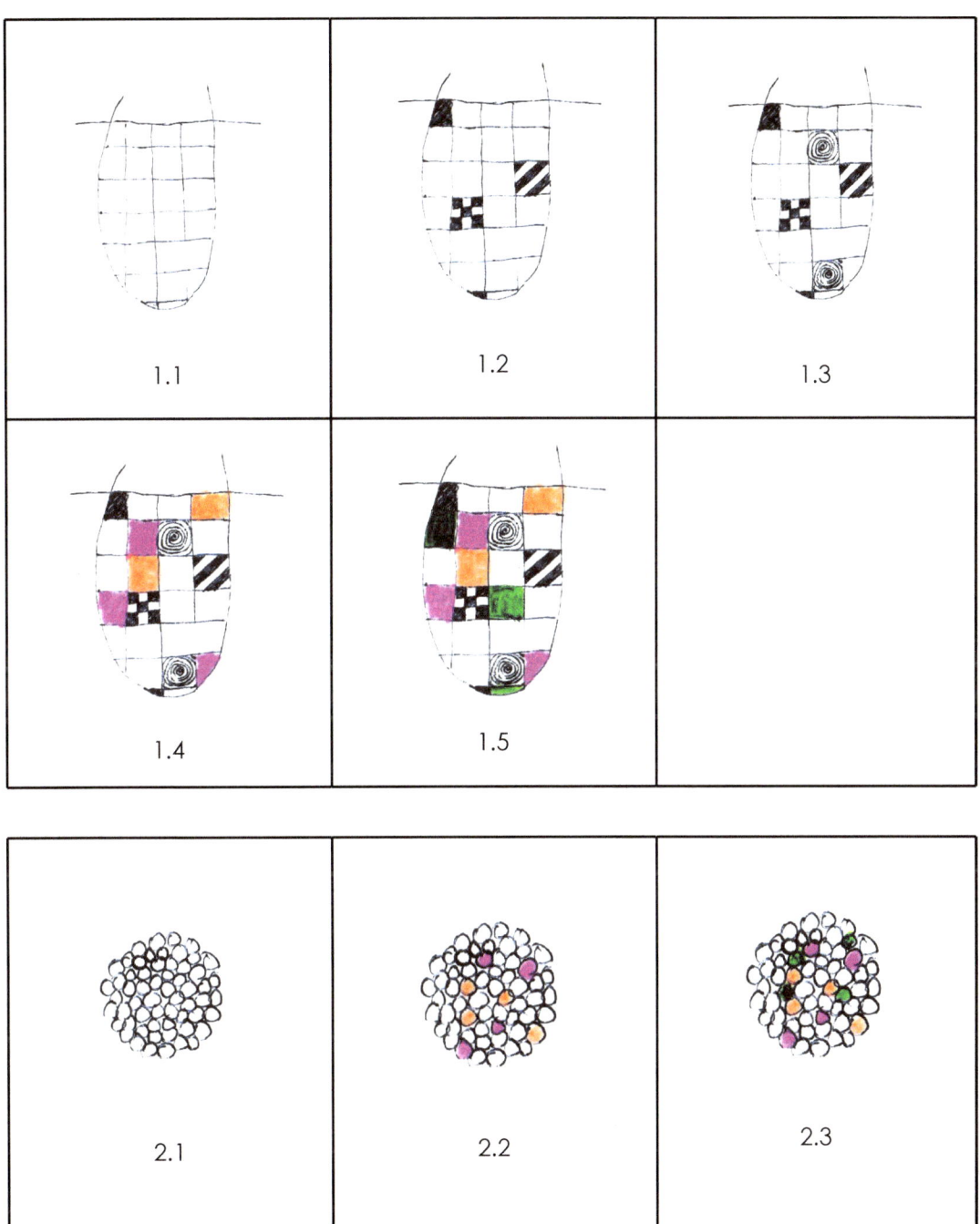

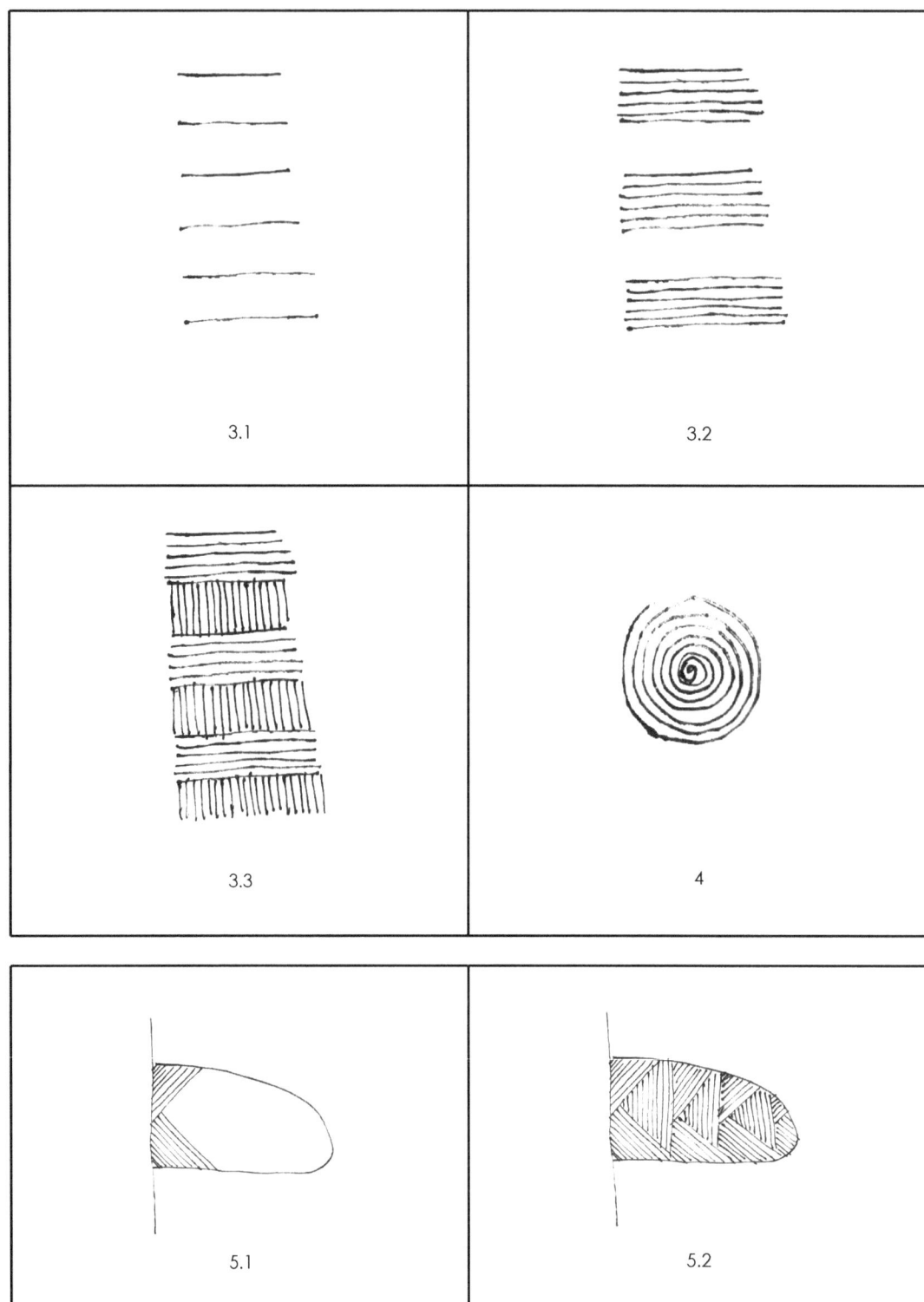

3.1

3.2

3.3

4

5.1

5.2

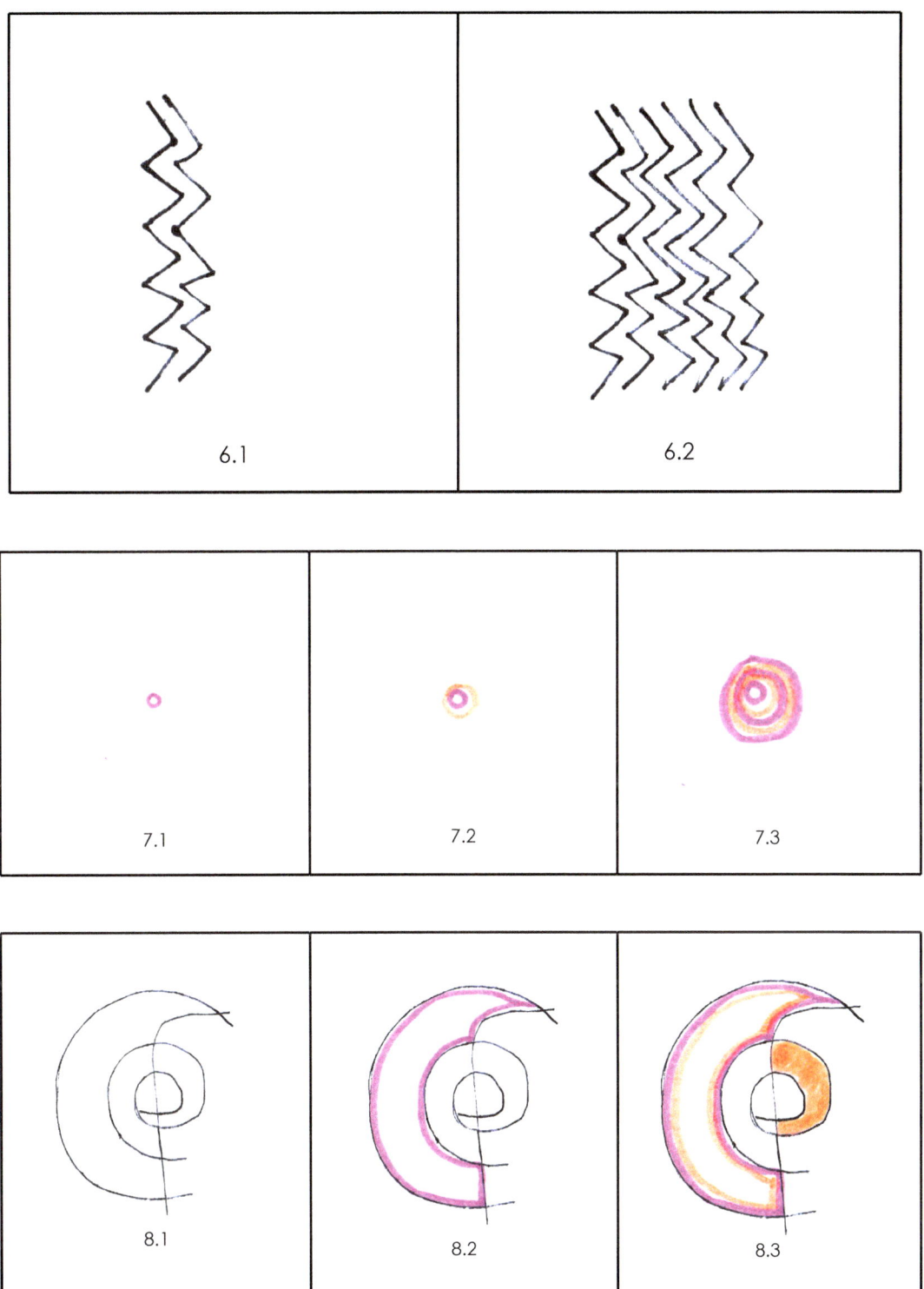

6.1

6.2

7.1

7.2

7.3

8.1

8.2

8.3

How to create NeoPopRealist color Abstract 2

The following pages will show step-by-step how to create color Abstract 2 that could be used as the background in NeoPopRealism drawing. Also it could be used as an independent ink design. Do not lose confidence when you enter a new space, drawing unlocks your creative spirit. When you draw, you express your ideas without words and in personal manner, and as a result, your work engaging people emotionally. Do not be a slave of your "left brain", be more intuitive, make connections, see bigger picture, trying to synthesize information in new ways. Create the harmony and balance in your compositions. Learn how this particular abstract was created. Every following picture includes new additional detail(s). The final abstract looks like this:

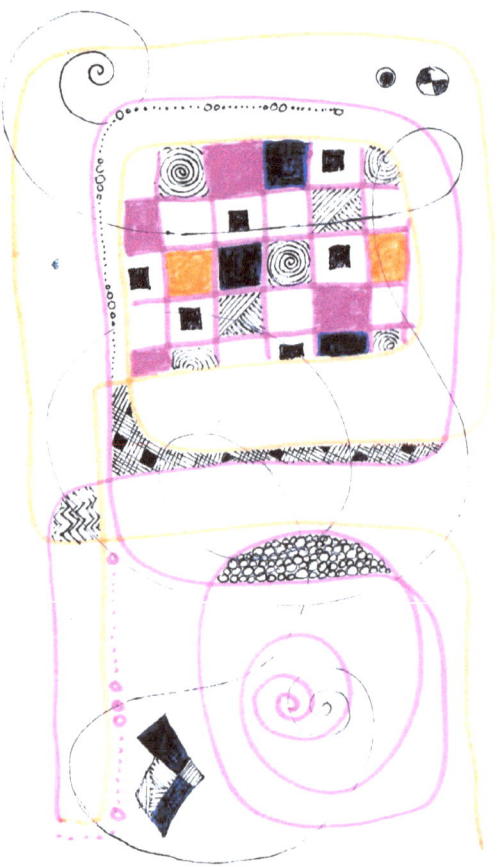

Abstract 2, Meditation, black ink pen & color markers on paper

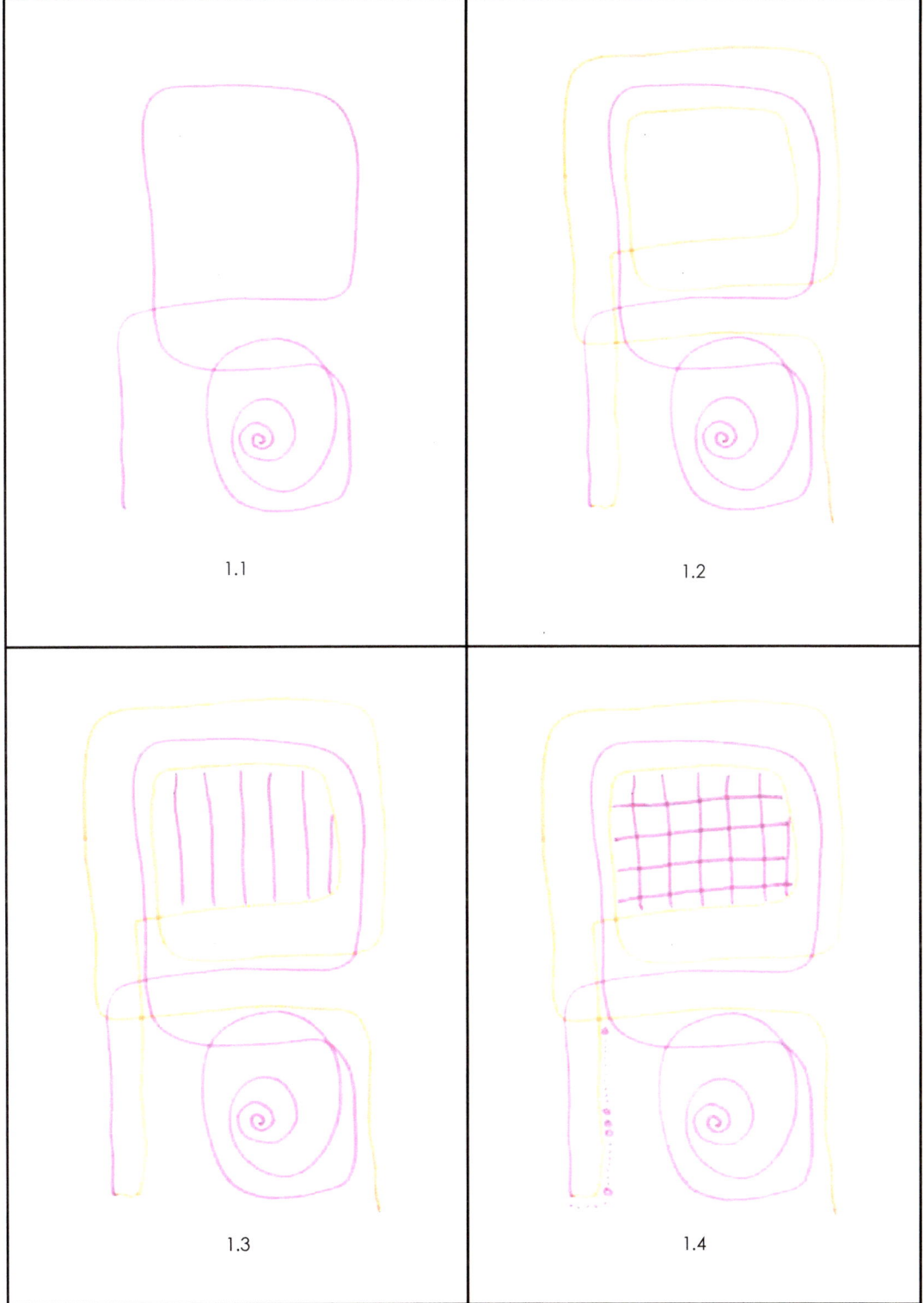

1.1

1.2

1.3

1.4

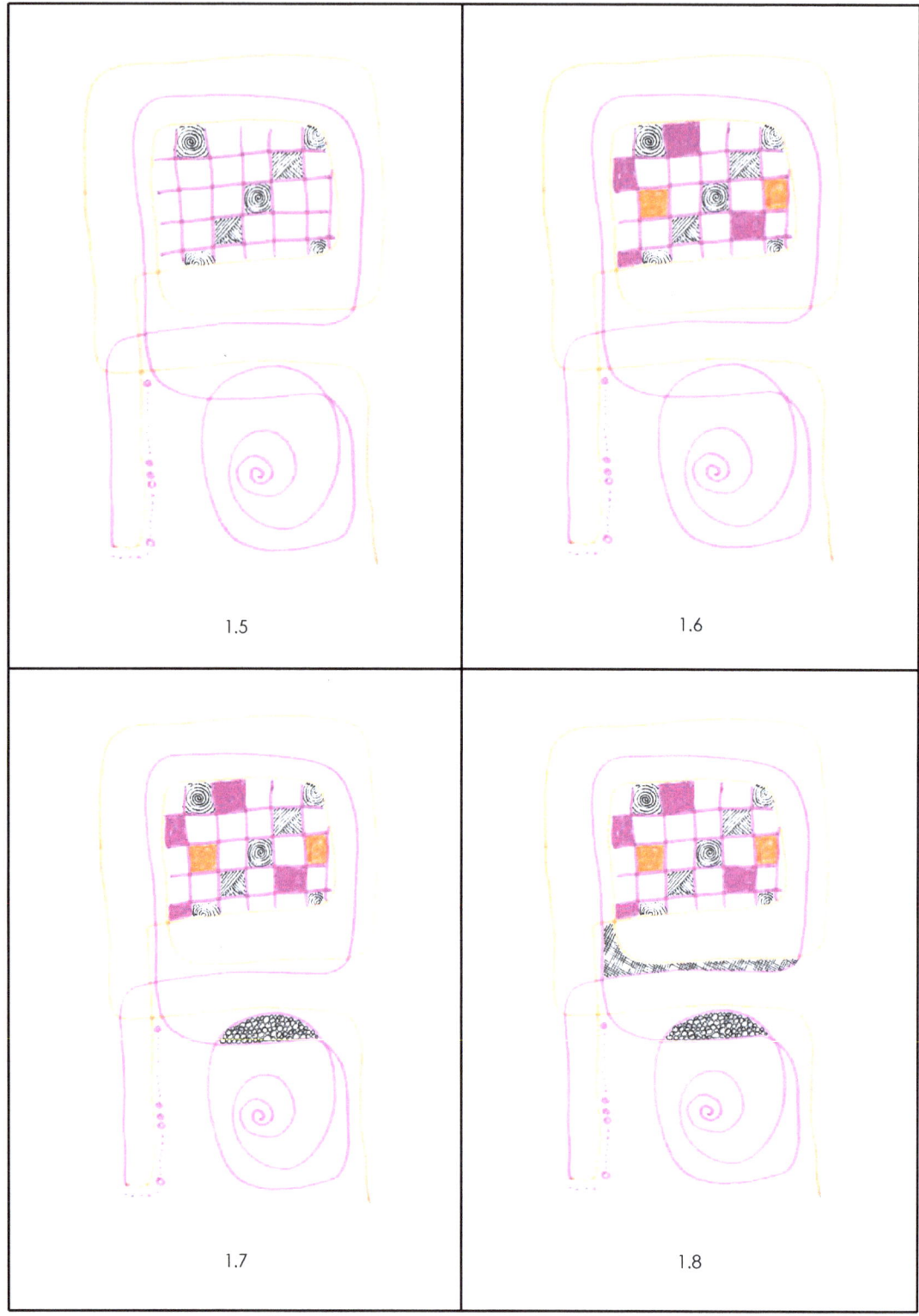

1.5

1.6

1.7

1.8

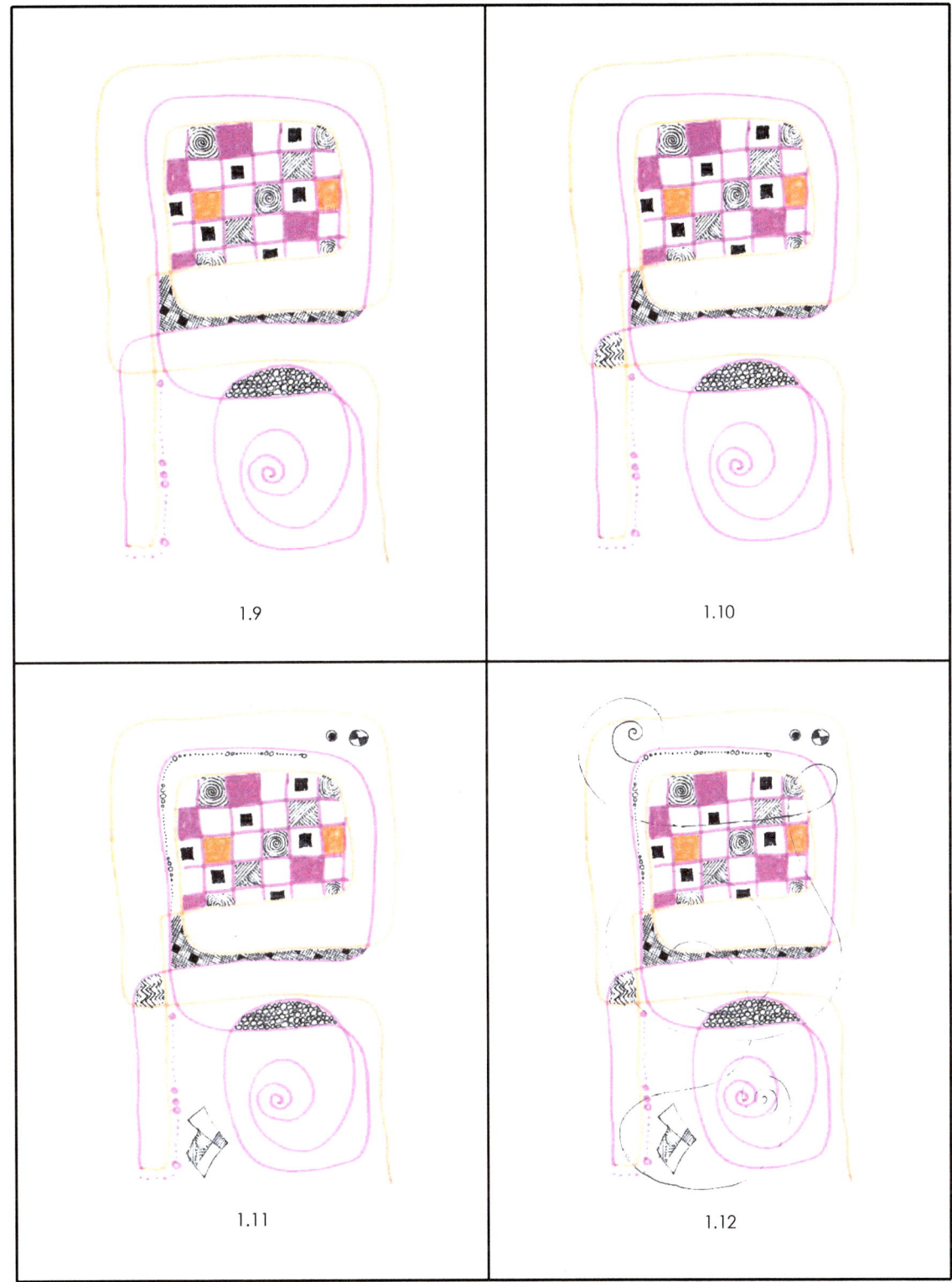

1.9

1.10

1.11

1.12

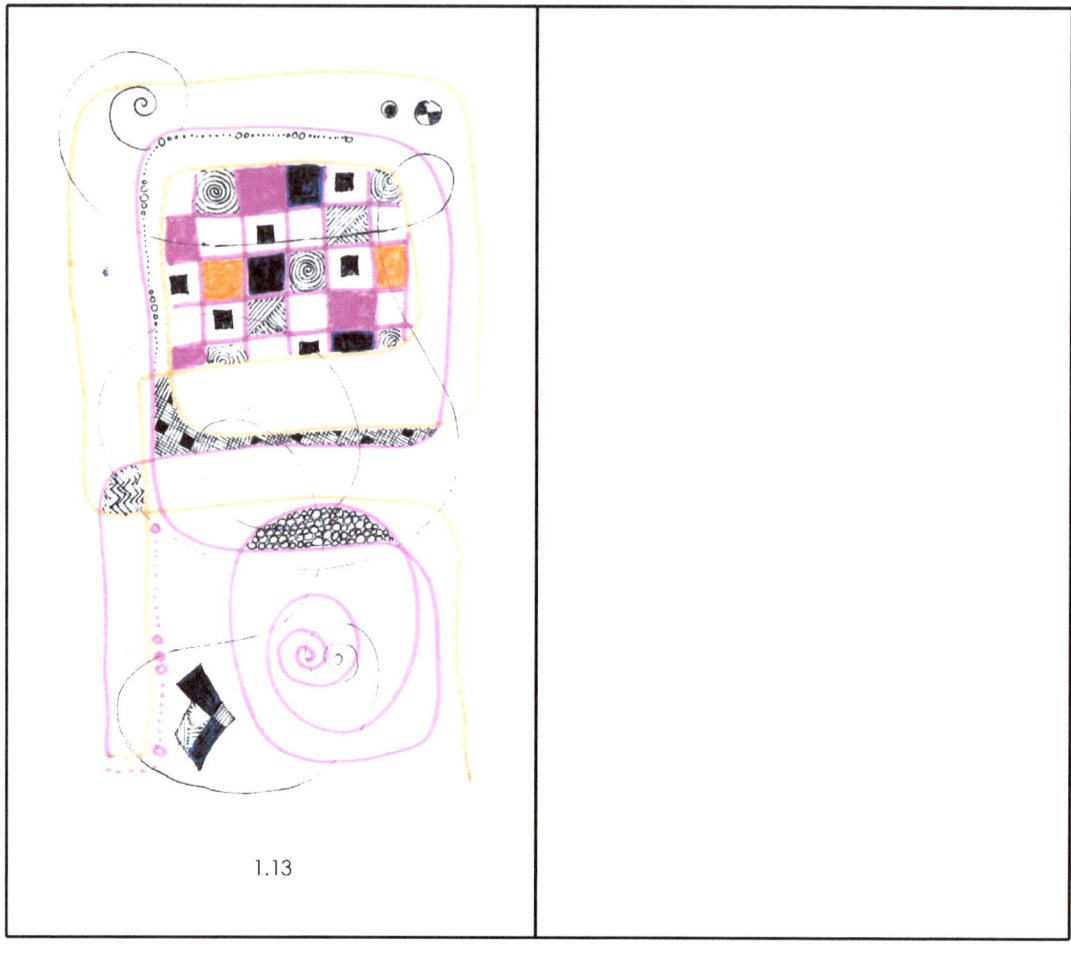

1.13

Pages 17-19 and 25-26 contain the visual instructions on how to draw repetitive patterns, used in Abstract 2. Every following image of each pattern includes new detail(s).

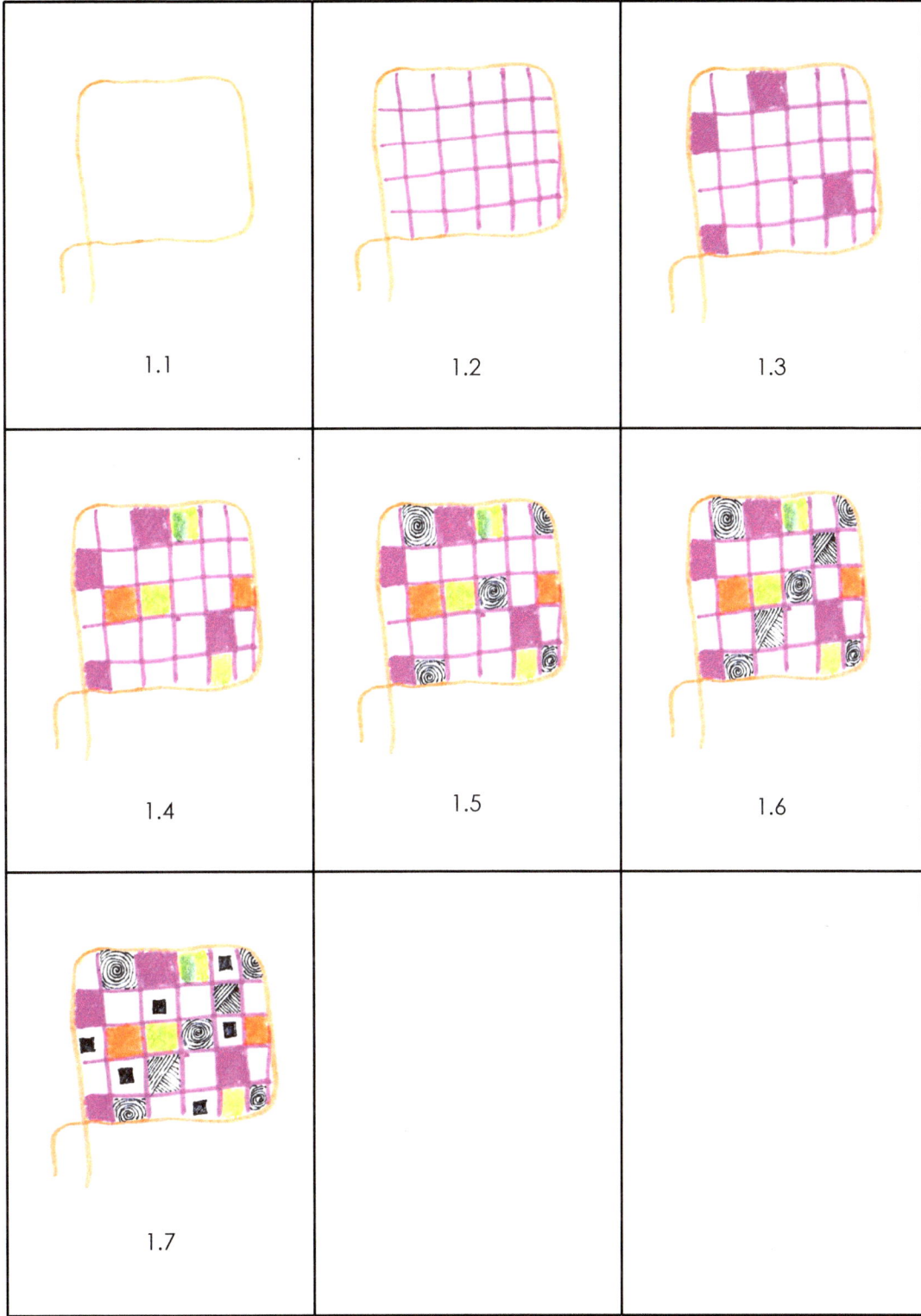

1.1

1.2

1.3

1.4

1.5

1.6

1.7

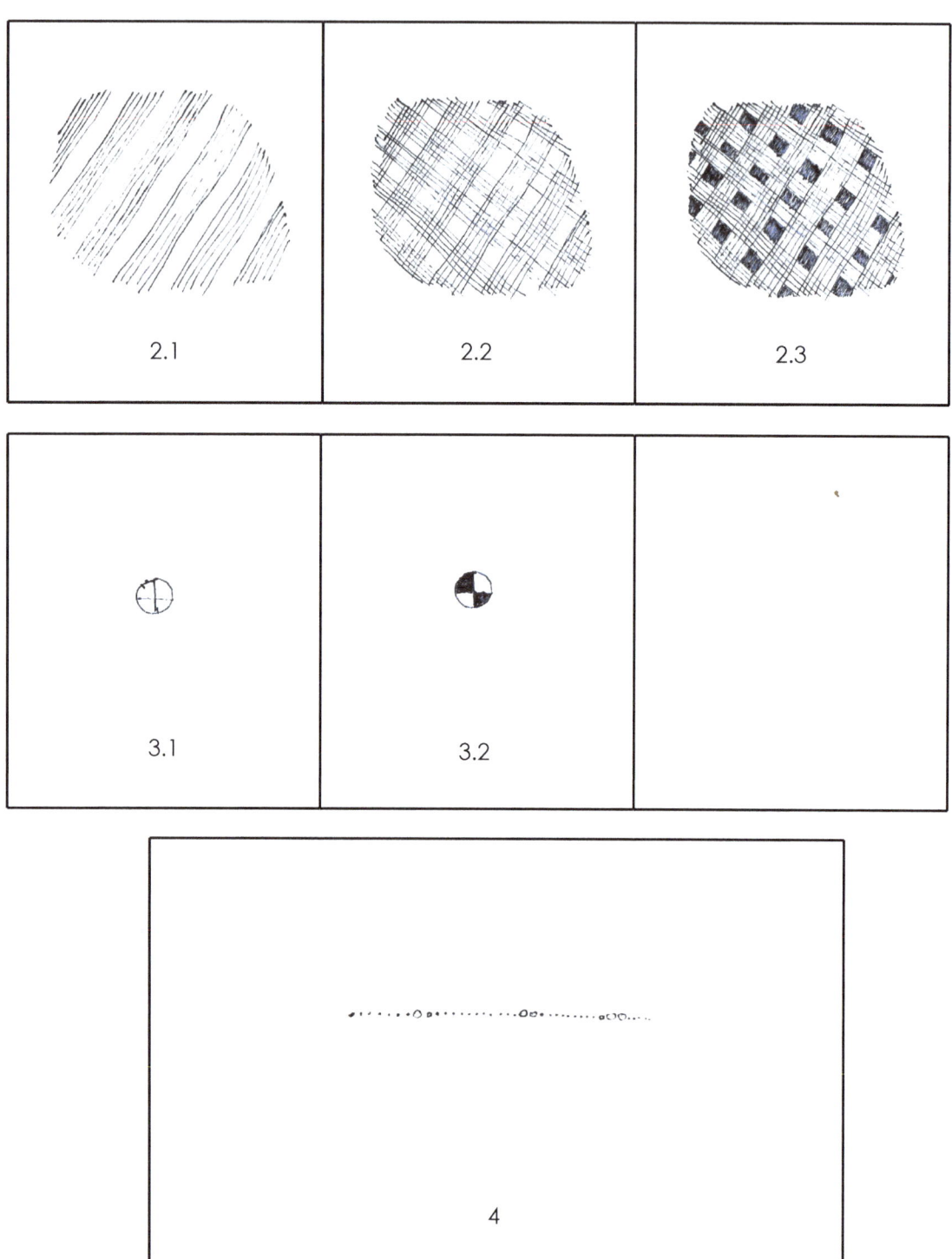

2.1

2.2

2.3

3.1

3.2

4

‖ ‖

Create abstracts with Nadia Russ

The following pages (28-37) invite you to draw abstracts with Nadia Russ here and now.

All you need is the black ink pen and markers or pens of different colors. Complete each drawing with additional lines. Fill some sections (or all) with different repetitive patterns.

When you draw repetitive patterns, in a few minutes you feel your breath as it enters and leaves your nostrils. You enter the meditative state of mind. Meditation is a positive brain-changing activity that increases your brain functions. It helps people who suffer from depression, anxiety, post-traumatic stress disorder and more. Meditation increases your memory and learning abilities. Through meditation you achieve sublime state of mind. There's strong connection between meditation, healthier immune system and happiness.

Stretch your imagination, try to reach new domains before seeking and analyze them in details. This drawing also will help you develop your artistic skills and intuition. Step-by-step you will learn how to create the balanced compositions.

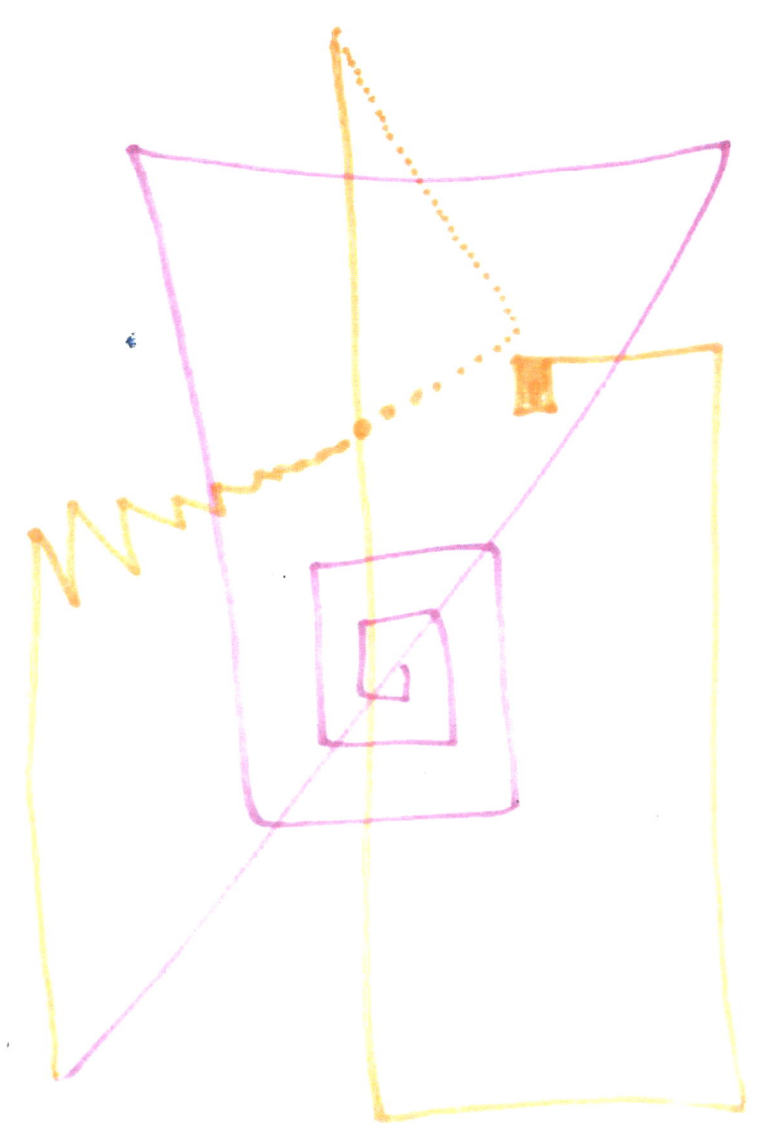

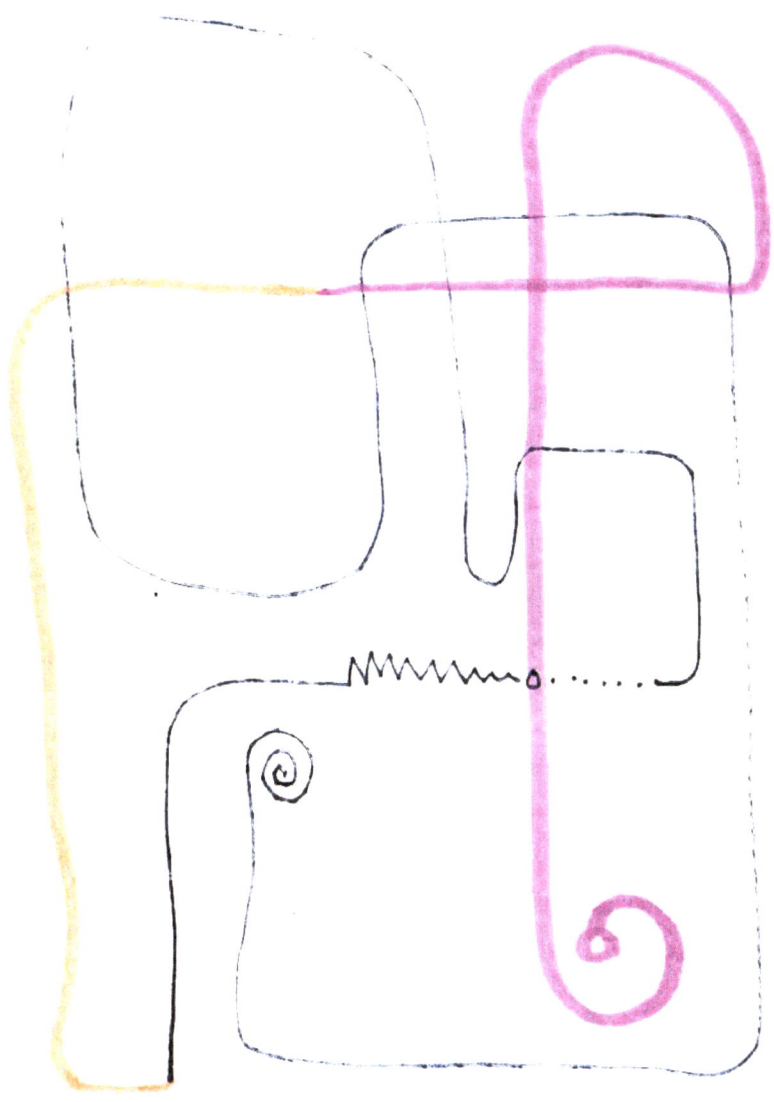

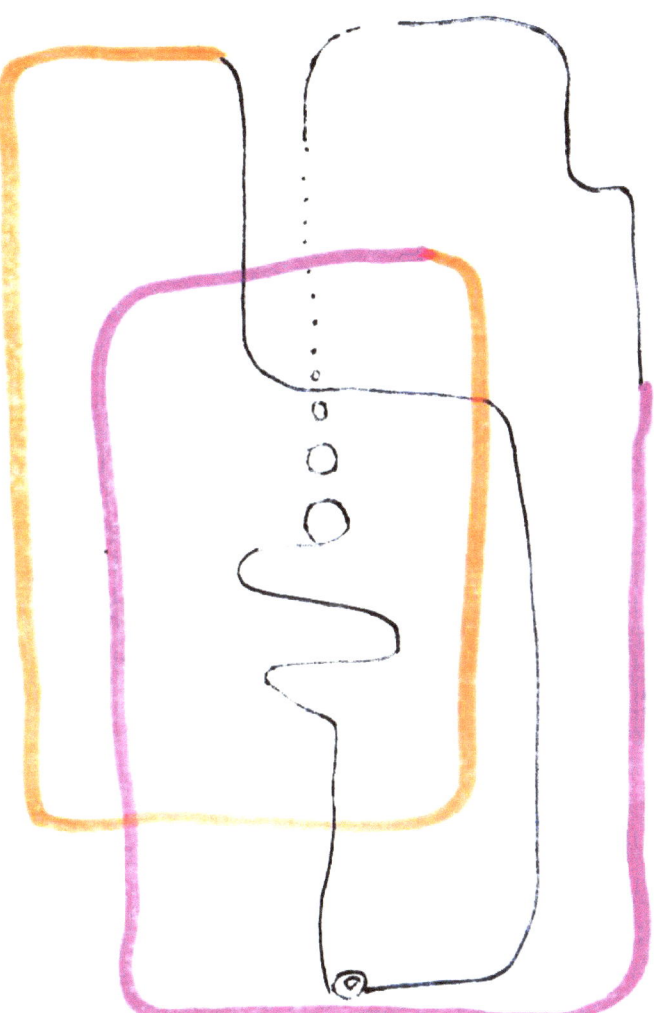

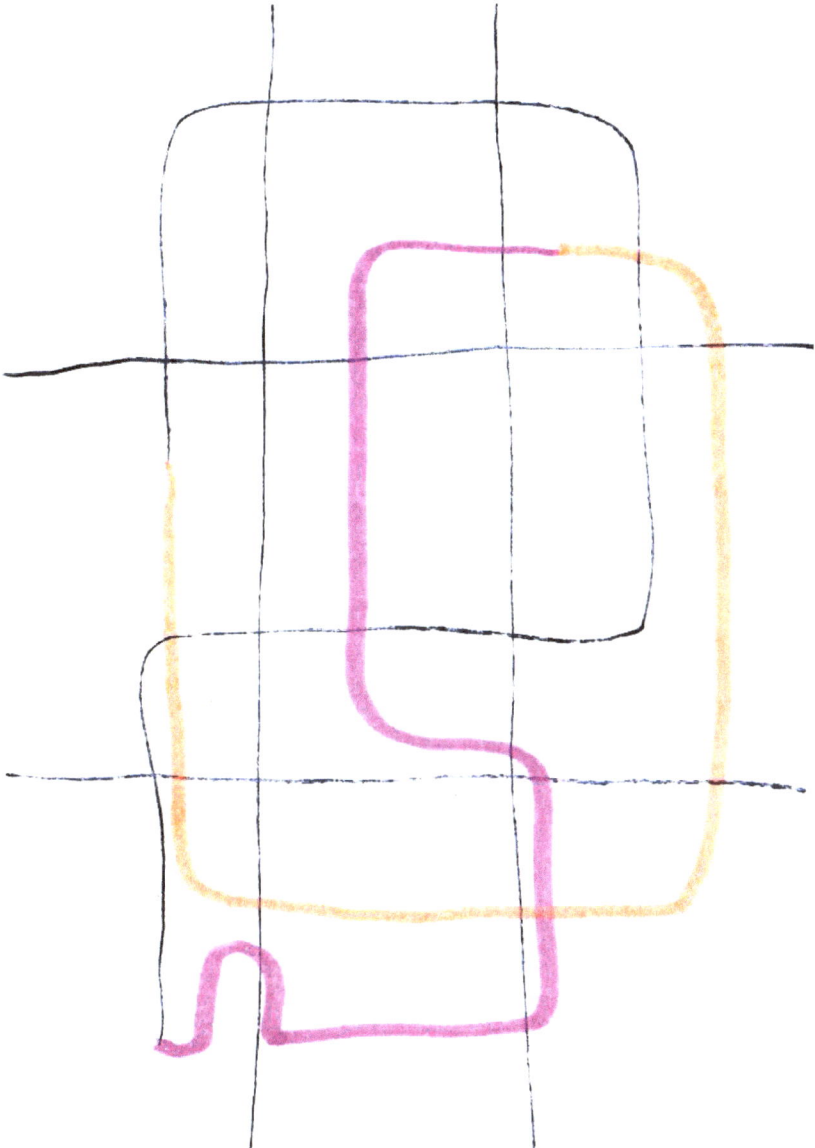

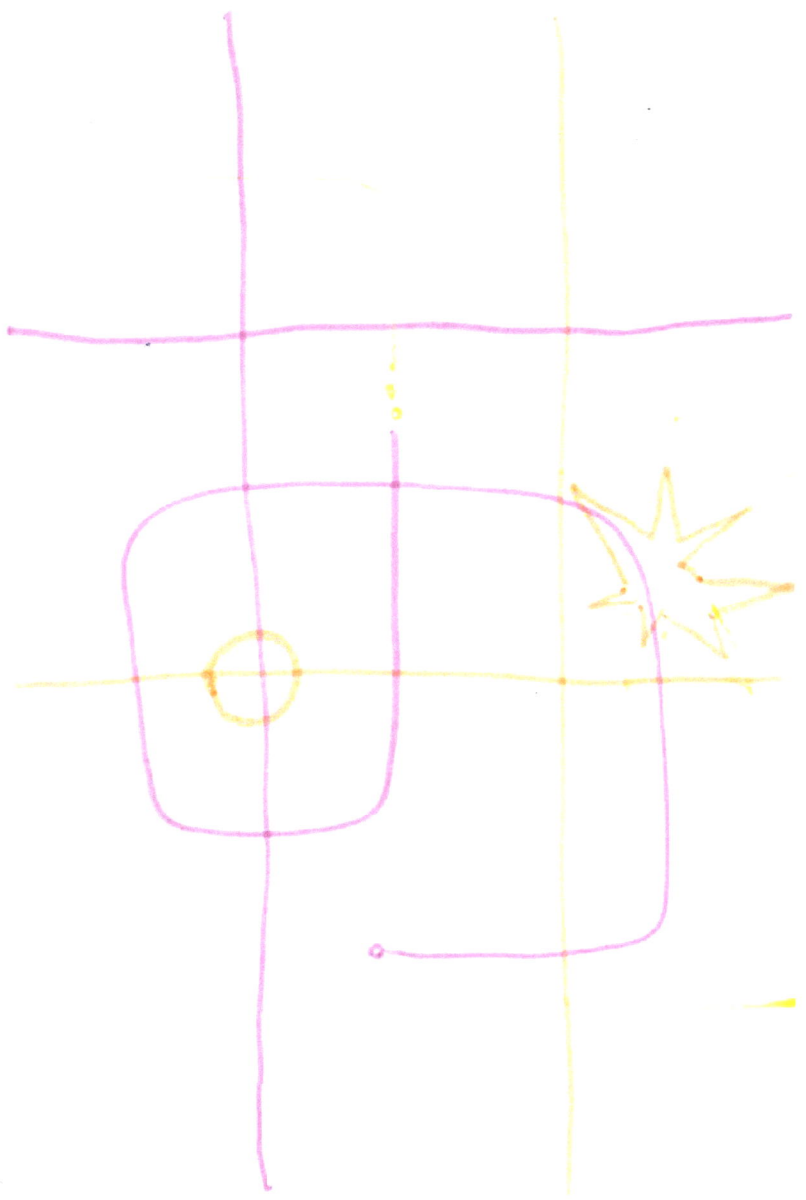

Create your repetitive patterns Gallery

The following pages invite you to create your personal repetitive patterns gallery here and now. Fill each section with different repetitive pattern. Use your imagination, make different combinations and variations of the line, circles, squares, dots, triangles, ovals, zigzag; twist and turn your line, following your creative instinct. This process will help you develop your artistic skills and imagination. You will use this patterns gallery later, when you will draw your future images.

1	2	3
4	5	6

7	8	9
10	11	12
13	14	15
16	17	18

19

20

21

22

23

24

25

26

27

28

29

30

31	32	33
34	35	36
37	38	39
40	41	42

43

44

45

46

47

48

49

50

51

52

53

54

Create your abstracts-drawings from the scratch

The following pages (49-55) are for you to create your NeoPopRealism color abstracts-drawings from the scratch. A few abstracts (pages 44-48) are here to give you some ideas about the variations. Do not copy them, they are copyrighted; use your imagination to create new abstracts. Use black ink pen and different colors pens/markers. Do not worry if you make a mistake. It will disappear with new repetitive patterns that will balance the whole composition. Concentrate on your drawing process, open your mind to possibilities. Remember that impossible is nothing. The repetitive patterns' drawing process will open you doors to the level of meditation and relaxation you never experienced before.

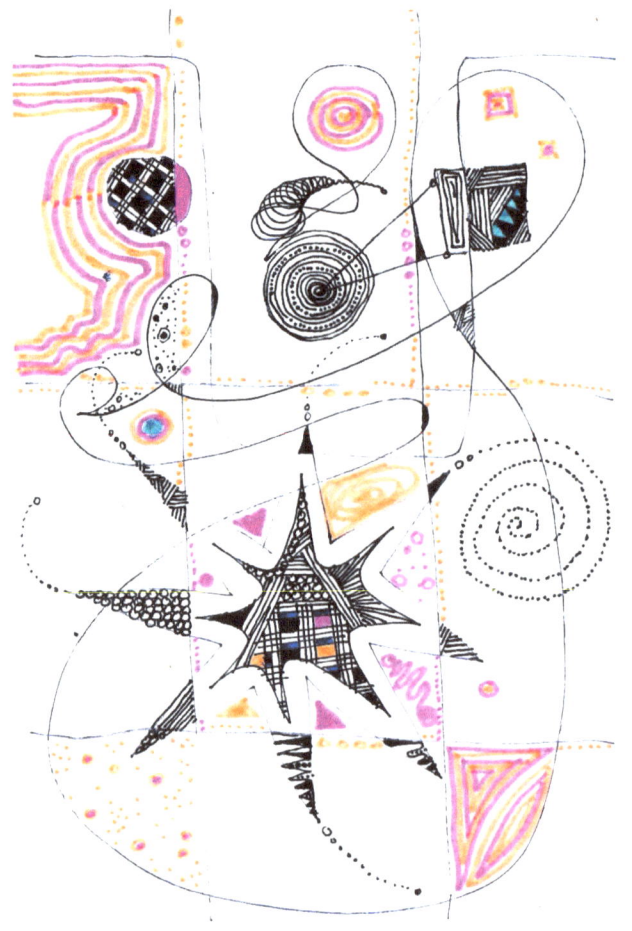

Nadia Russ, *Abstract 3, Meditation*, black ink pen & color markers on paper

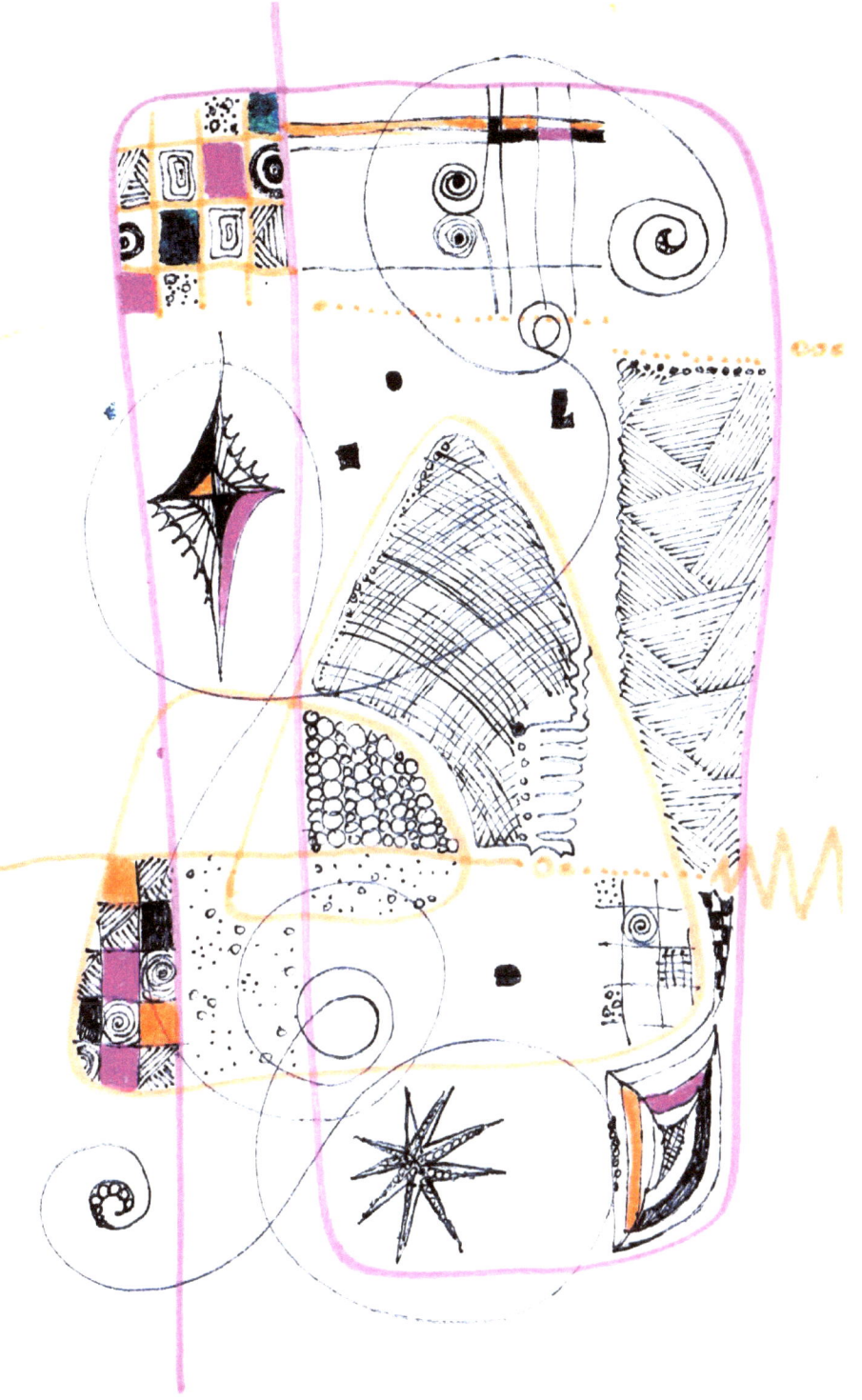

Nadia Russ, *Abstract 4, Meditation*, black ink pen & color markers on paper

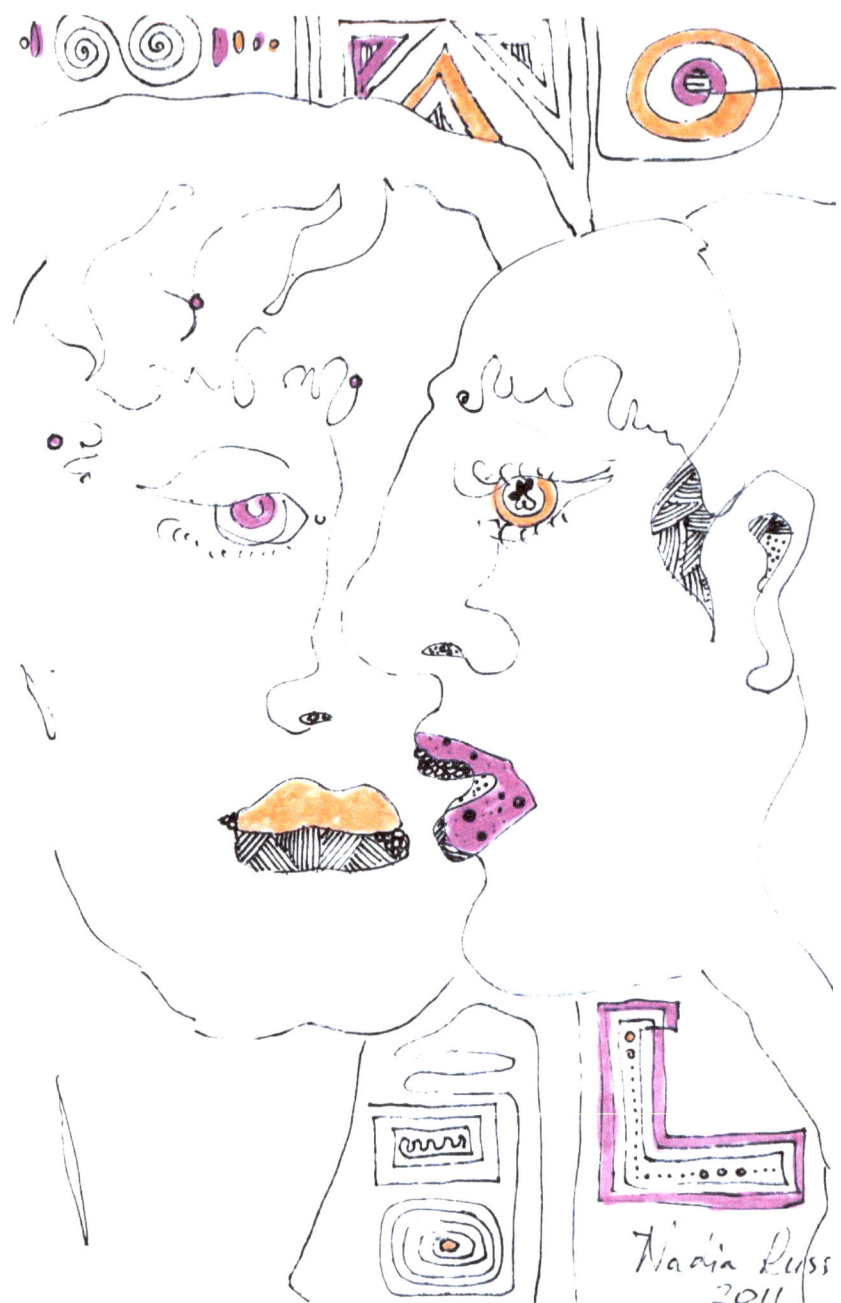

Nadia Russ, *Faces 1*, black ink pen & color markers on paper, 5.5"x8.5"

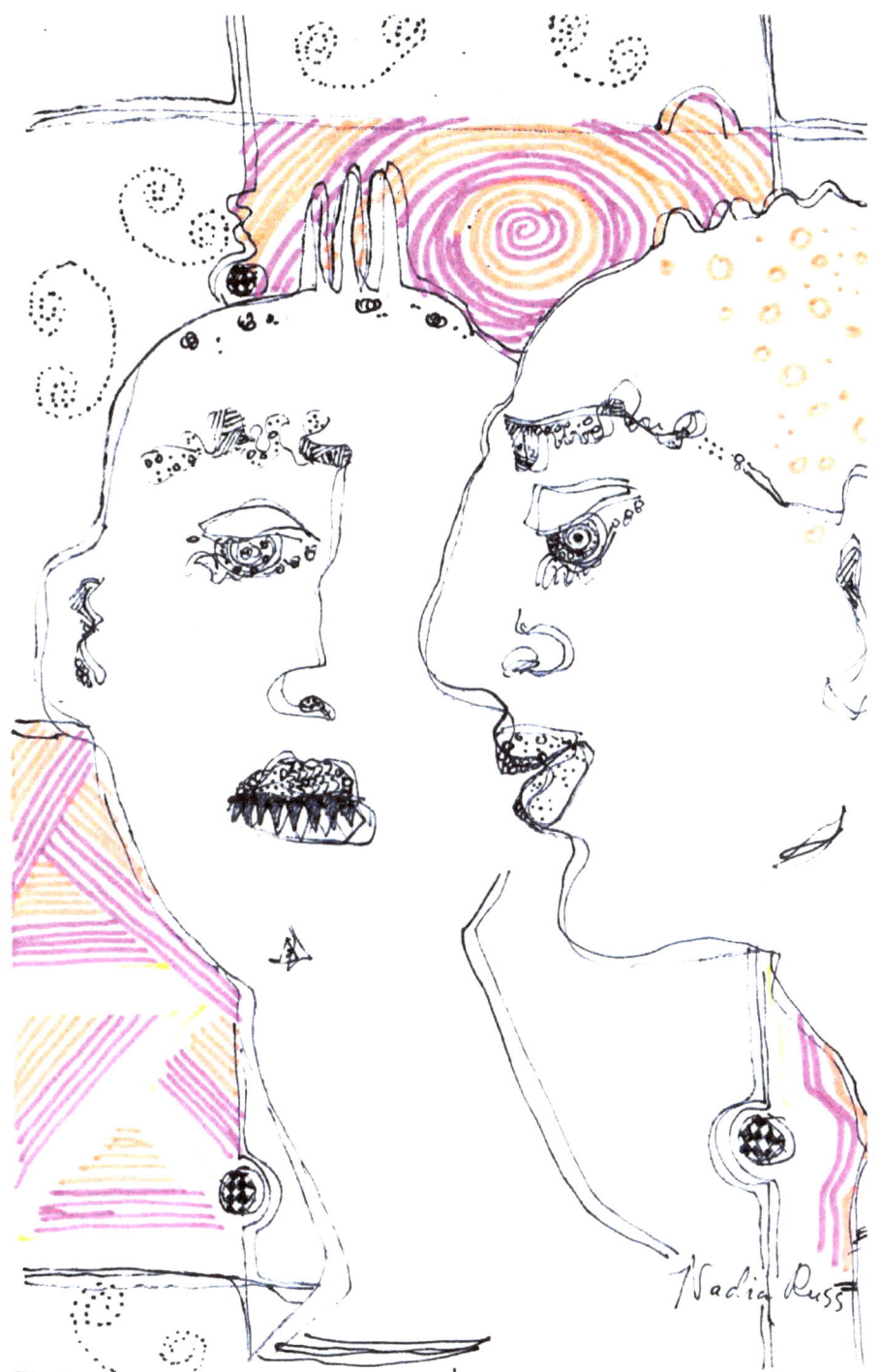

Nadia Russ, *Faces 2*, black ink pen & color markers on paper, 5.5"x8.5"

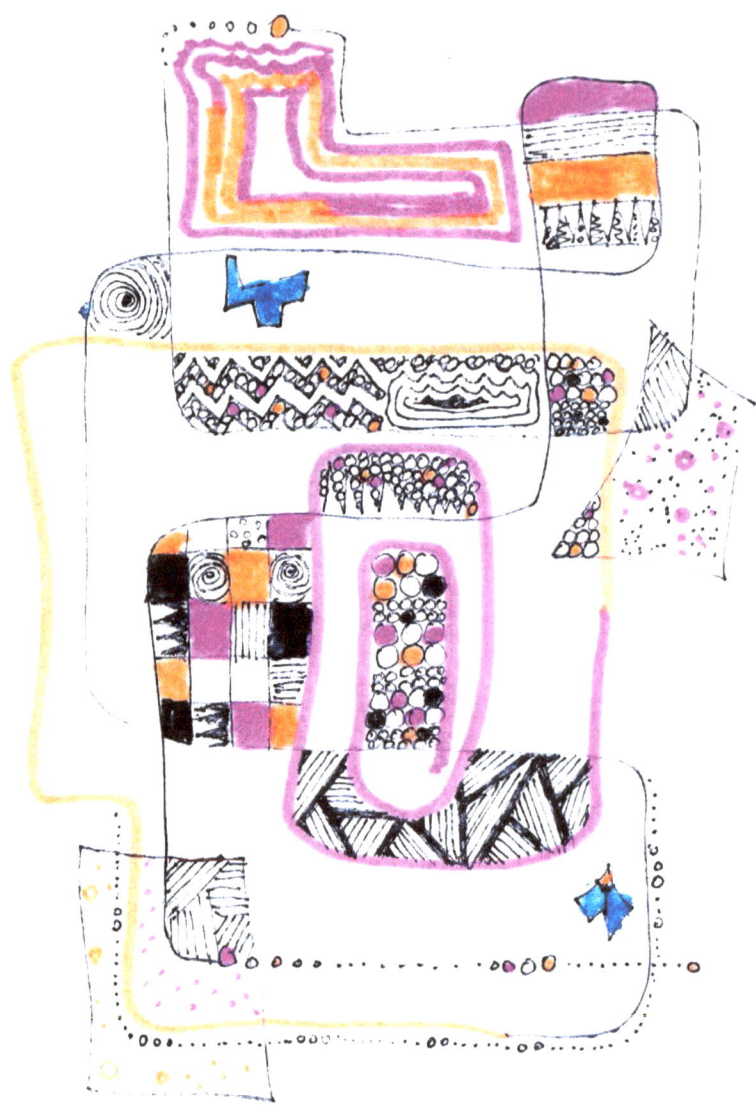

Nadia Russ, *Abstract 5, Meditation, black ink pen & color markers* on paper

About NeoPopRealism creator Nadia Russ

Nadia Russ (aka Nadejda Maloletneva) was born into a former professional military officer's family. As a child, she began studying art from famous masters of the past through art books and reproductions, which her mother Vera was collecting in their home. Nadia daily heard about and saw the reproductions of works of Leonardo da Vinci, Michelangelo, Rafael, contemporary Russian artists such as Petrov-Vodkin.

She began painting and drawing seriously in 1989. A few months later, her first ink drawings were exhibited in a group exhibition in famous Moscow's Manege and later, in other Moscow's art galleries. In 1992, she successfully showed her work in New York City.

In 1996-2000, Nadia resided in the Bahamas, where her work gained some special brightness. There, she got her pseudonym to her original 'Nadejda Maloletneva', which was easier to pronounce - 'Nadia Russ'. In 2000-2001, in Xanadu hotel, she operated her Art Gallery Club 13.

In 2000, she moved to the United States, where she lives up until present. January 4, 2003, Nadia Russ created a word NeoPopRealism and manifested internationally new style of visual arts which combines the brightness and simplicity of Pop Art with deep and psychological realism and has graphic nature. Her artworks are in private and permanent public collections including MOYA - Museum of Young Art in Vienna (Austria), Simferopol and Sumy Art Museums in Ukraine, Kinsey Institute of Indiana University (USA), Ukrainian Museum in New York City (USA), WEAM - World Erotic Art Museum in Miami (USA), Schacknow Museum of Fine Arts (USA), Historical Museum of Fort Lauderdale (USA), Lebedyn and Konotop Art Museums (Ukraine), D. Burliuk Foundation (Ukraine), and other.

In 2008-2010, Nadia Russ founded and juried Int'l NeoPopRealism Starz Art competitions. She authored a few art-related books such as "NeoPopRealism Starz: 21st Century ART" two volumes, "New Millennium ART", "Fort Lauderdale 100: A Must-Have Collector's Edition." She is the founder (2007) of the *NeoPopRealism Journal & Wonderpedia*, publications online, dedicated to arts, culture, books, news, celebrities and more. Nadia Russ lives in New York City and Florida. Visit her website at www.nadiaruss.com.

Conclusion

What is Art?

Now, when you have learned how to draw the NeoPopRealism abstract images, you might have your answer to this open question. We'll be happy to hear from you, e-mail us to neopoprealism1@yahoo.com. Also, if you have a blog, post there images of your NeoPopRealism ink drawings and a story how you learned to draw them. And, please, mention there this book with NeoPopRealism creator Nadia Russ. Have a wonderful journey to the world of NeoPopRealism!

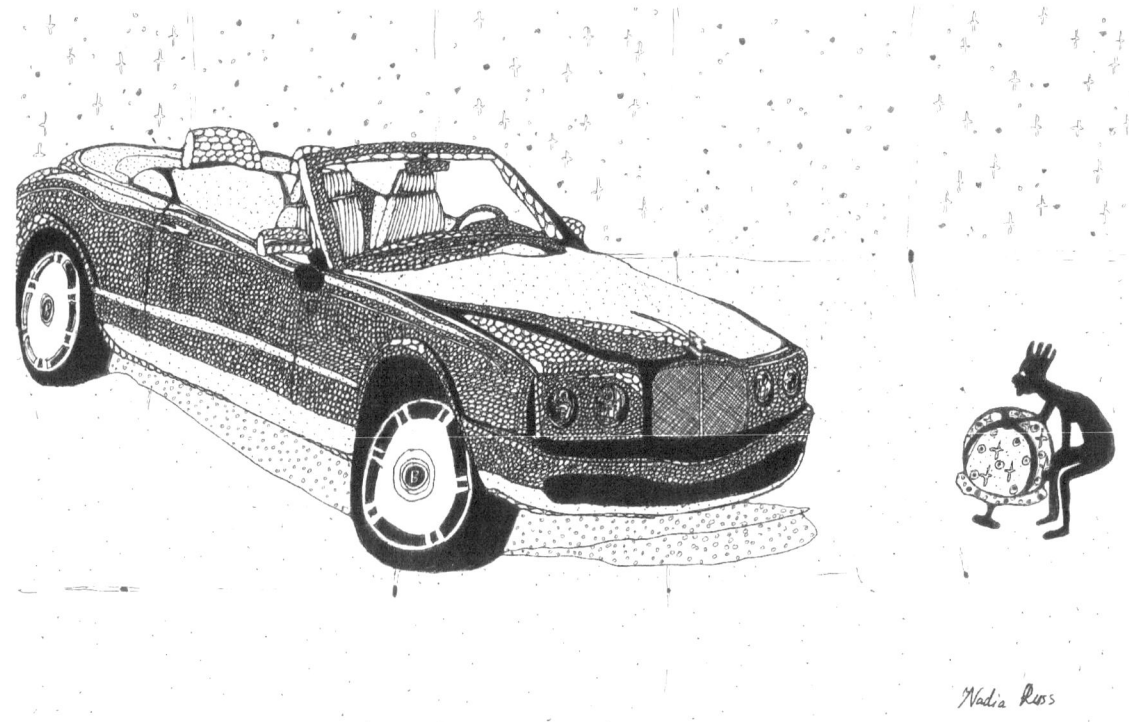

Nadia Russ, *Bentley Convertible*, black Ink, with lipstick & nail polish insertions, paper, 11x17, 2006. Collections of MOYA, Museum of Young Art, Vienna (Austria)

NeoPopRealism ten canons for happier life

1. Be beautiful.
2. Be creative and productive; never stop studying and learning.
3. Be peace-loving, positive-minded.
4. Do not accept communist philosophy.
5. Be free-minded, do the best you can to move the world to peace and harmony.
6. Be family oriented, self-disciplined.
7. Be free spirited. Follow your dreams, if they are not destructive, but constructive.
8. Believe in god. God is one; it is harmony and striving for perfection.
9. Be supportive to those who need you, be generous.
10. Create your life as a great adventurous story.

Created by Nadia Russ in 2004

Additional books - teaching / learning material on NeoPopRealism Ink drawing for adults, teenagers and children published in 2011

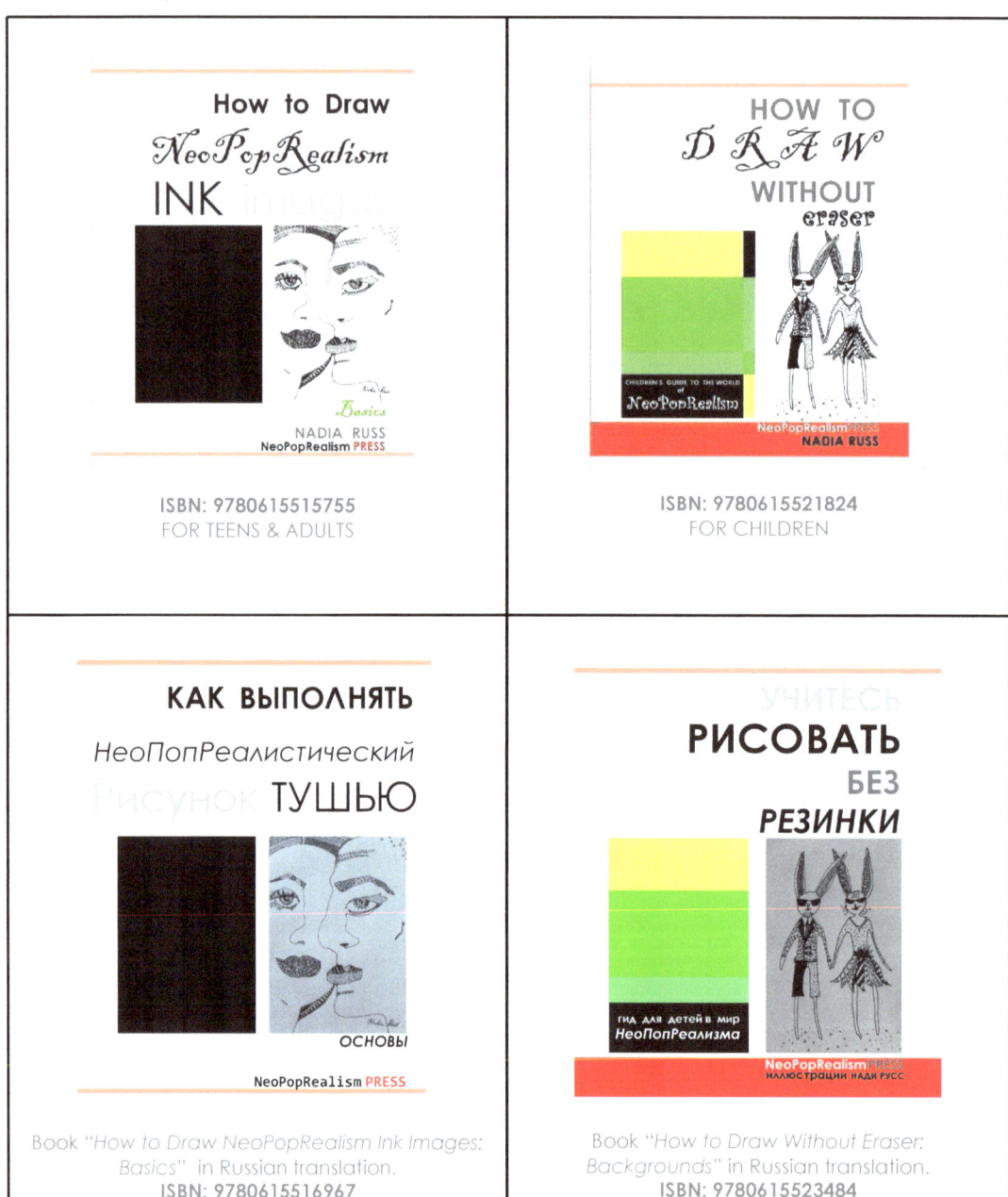

ISBN: 9780615515755
FOR TEENS & ADULTS

ISBN: 9780615521824
FOR CHILDREN

Book "How to Draw NeoPopRealism Ink Images: Basics" in Russian translation.
ISBN: 9780615516967

Book "How to Draw Without Eraser: Backgrounds" in Russian translation.
ISBN: 9780615523484

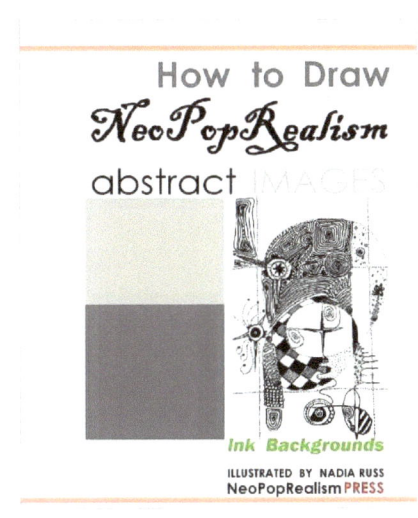

ISBN: 9780615527437
FOR TEENS & ADULTS

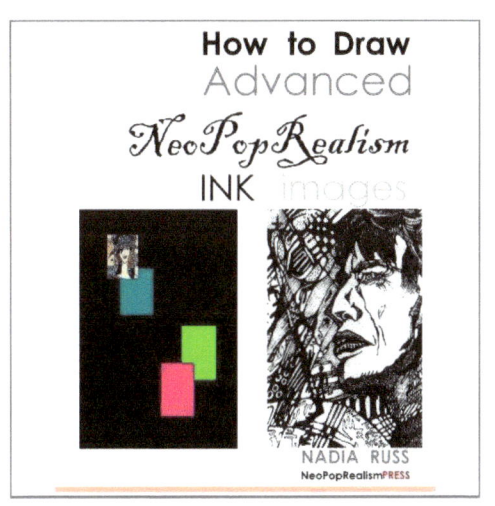

ISBN: 9780615569758
FOR TEENS & ADULTS

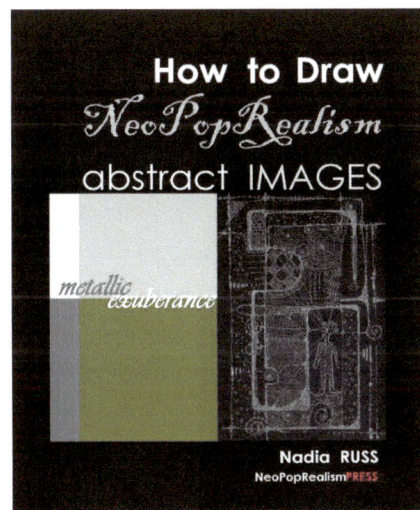

ISBN: 9780615560991
FOR TEENS & ADULTS

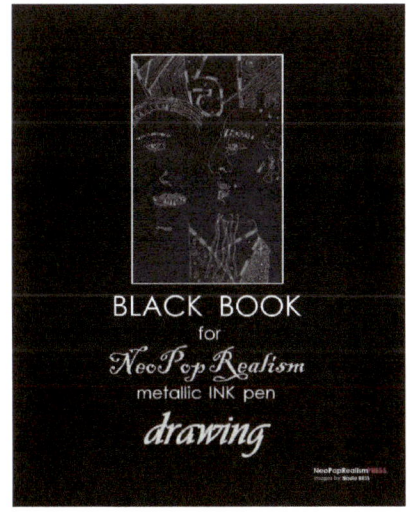

ISBN:9780615561028
FOR ALL AGES & LEVELS

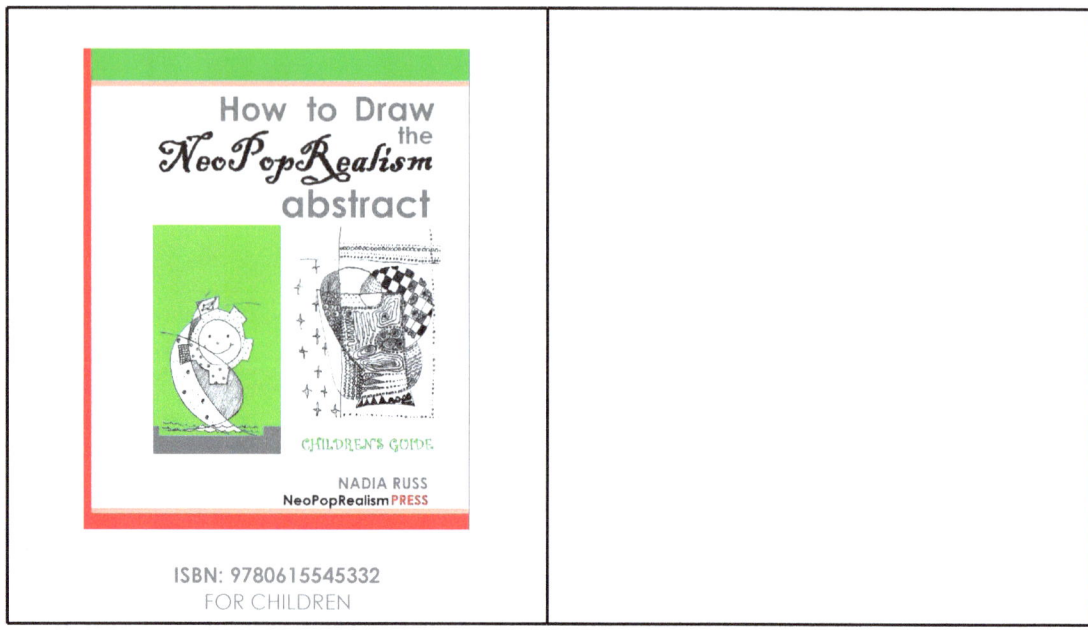

ISBN: 9780615545332
FOR CHILDREN

How to Draw NeoPopRealism Color Abstract Images: Ink Backgrounds

The following collection of the ink drawings by Nadia Russ will give you some ideas about how you can use repetitive patterns in drawings that include not only the abstract designs, but faces, figures and anything else. Use your imagination and your creative abilities. You also can use the repetitive patterns in your realistic drawings. Do not copy these images, they are copyrighted; use your skills and imagination to create something new, never seen before, this what art is about - uniqueness. Use black ink pen combining it with different colors' pens/markers as you saw on the previous pages of this book. The next book will teach you how to create the NeoPopRealism color realistic images.

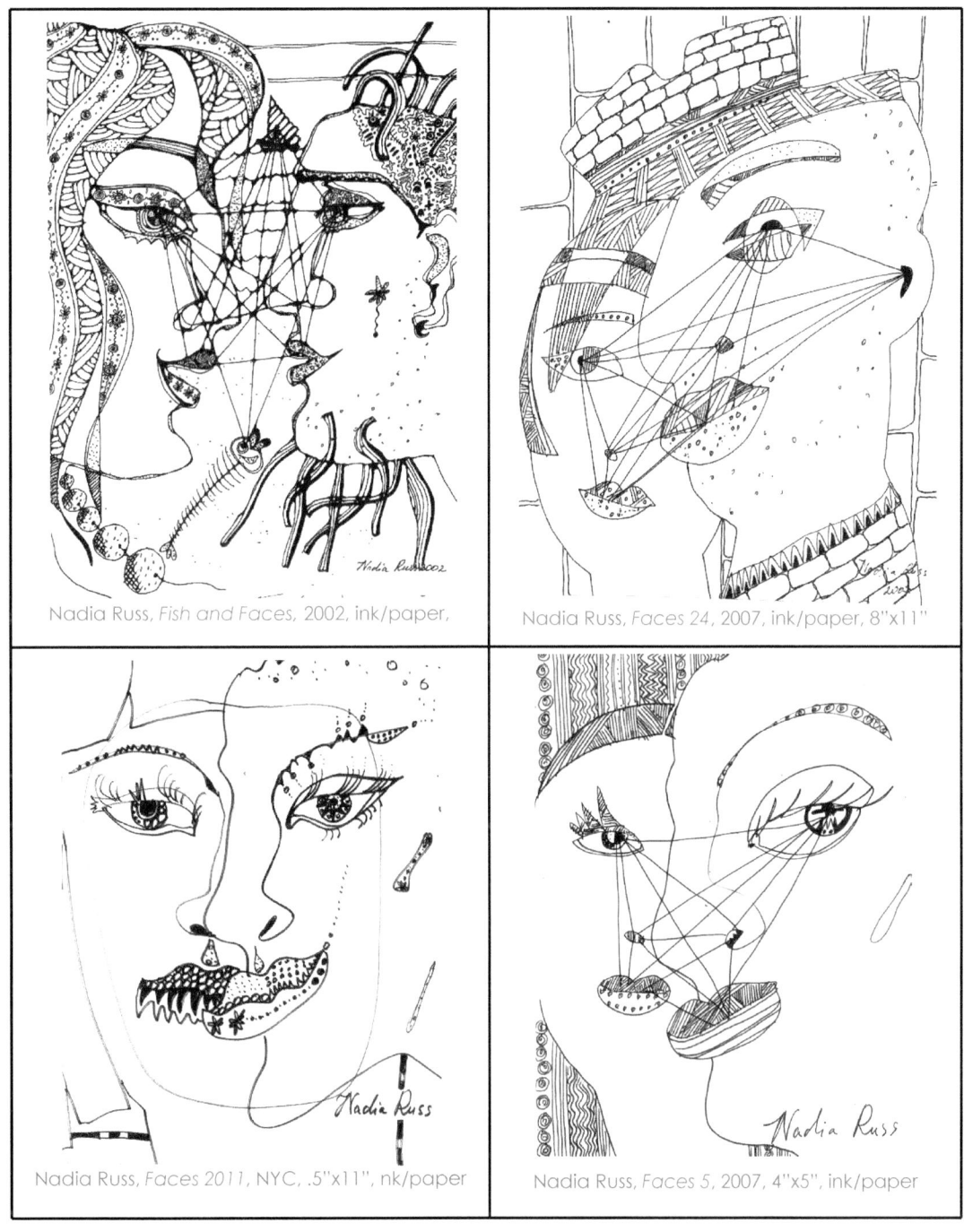

Nadia Russ, *Fish and Faces*, 2002, ink/paper,

Nadia Russ, *Faces 24*, 2007, ink/paper, 8"x11"

Nadia Russ, *Faces 2011*, NYC, .5"x11", nk/paper

Nadia Russ, *Faces 5*, 2007, 4"x5", ink/paper

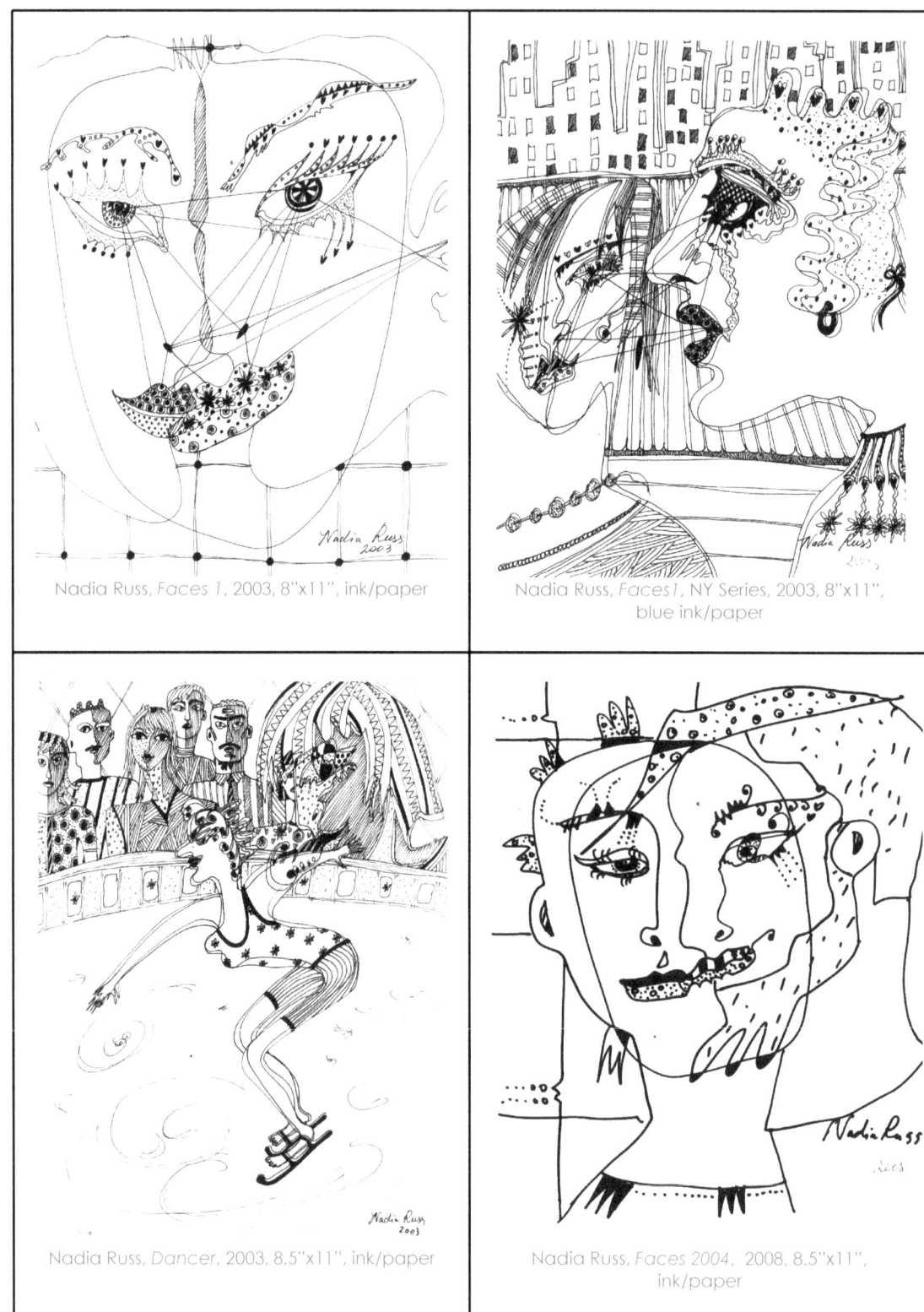

Nadia Russ, *Faces 1*, 2003, 8"x11", ink/paper

Nadia Russ, *Faces1*, NY Series, 2003, 8"x11", blue ink/paper

Nadia Russ, *Dancer*, 2003, 8.5"x11", ink/paper

Nadia Russ, *Faces 2004*, 2008, 8.5"x11", ink/paper

Use following pages for drawing NeoPopRealist images.

www.ingramcontent.com/pod-product-compliance
Lightning Source LLC
Chambersburg PA
CBHW051027180526
45172CB00002B/500